BEYOND ADVENTURE

BEYOND ADVENTURE

REFLECTIONS FROM THE WILDERNESS: AN INNER JOURNEY

by
Colin Mortlock

Foreword by Chris Bonington

2 POLICE SQUARE, MILNTHORPE, CUMBRIA, LA7 7PY
www.cicerone.co.uk

*This book is dedicated to the beauty
and mystery of wild Nature*

Wild Nature provided the inspiration for this book. For this reason, I am deeply grateful to all those people who have helped me to adventure in the wild, and to those who have aided my understanding of such experiences.

From first ideas to completed manuscript has not been easy. I would like to thank everyone who constructively commented on the initial drafts, in particular Ian Bownes, John Carnie, Rob Collister, Robin Hodgkin, Alison Morton and my eldest daughter, Vember.

Special thanks go to my editor, Jim Perrin. His professional skill has been impressive. I have appreciated his perception, his style of persuasion and his belief in what I was trying to say.

Special thanks also go to my wife, Annette. She played a key role in the research and editing process as well as taking on the major task of word-processing. With Jim and Annette's assistance I eventually came to enjoy the preparation of the final draft.

Finally, I wish to thank all the team at my publisher, Cicerone, for their support, enthusiasm and positive input from start to finish.

© Colin Mortlock 2001

ISBN 1 85284 332 2

A catalogue record for this book is available from the British Library.

Colin Mortlock is also the author of *The Adventure Alternative* (1984), published by Cicerone Press.

Front cover: Sunset over the Western Isles, Scotland

CONTENTS

Foreword by Chris Bonington 6

Preface 7

Introduction 9

Chapter 1: Self 12

Chapter 2: Deeper into Self 21

Chapter 3: The Impact of Other People 27

Chapter 4: The Impact of Nature 36

Chapter 5: Sea Kayaking and Alaska 50

Chapter 6: Elemental Experiences 59

Chapter 7: Wild Flowers and Trekking 69

Chapter 8: Further Reflections 75

Chapter 9: A Pilgrim in the Wild 81

Chapter 10: Seeking Unity with Nature 89

Chapter 11: Inner Resources 98

Chapter 12: A Framework of Values 110

Epilogue: Back to the Wilderness 120

Endnotes 122

Bibliography 126

Appendix A: Basic Beliefs 129

Appendix B: Outdoor Education 131

Appendix C: Further Notes on Inner Resources 132

Appendix D: Inner Self and Ideal Self 134

Colin Mortlock 136

Comments about Beyond Adventure 137

FOREWORD

This is an intriguing book that not only digs deep into why and how we go adventuring but also challenges many pre-conceptions. When reading *Beyond Adventure*, I frequently found myself empathising with Colin, as he explored ideas and feelings that I had touched upon in my own journey but had not thought through or expressed in depth.

He discovers the joy of physical expression when everything seems to flow together – something I, as a climber, have experienced. Just a few times, when I have committed myself to a series of moves, often away from any kind of protection and with the minimum of holds, I have felt as one with the rock under my fingers and toes. There is that total concentration that banishes the fear one might initially have felt – and then, the moves complete, the pitch climbed, a sense of euphoria that develops into an inner peace. I remember another occasion, on my way down from the top camp on the South West Face of Everest in 1975. We had carried the gear that Doug Scott and Dougal Haston needed for their summit bid and had done all that we could to help them. Once again I had a profound sense of contentment at a job well done, heightened by my appreciation for my fellow expedition members and the extraordinary focus and unity we had achieved as a group.

One can't and won't want to skim through this book. There are so many levels within it; each level helps one to understand one's own motivation and what one gets from adventure at different stages of one's life. So much is about balance – the balance between the ego or ambition that drives most of us and that more selfless sense of oneness with our environment that I believe gives the greatest long-term satisfaction. This of course can be seen both in a personal and a global sense, which is particularly relevant today in a society that seems more and more bent on instant personal gratification – be it in having adventure delivered quickly and easily on a plate or in our attitude to the environment and rest of the world.

Colin, in his own perceptive and, I suspect at times, painful honesty of self-analysis, enables all of us to learn more about what we gain not only from adventure and the outdoors, but from life itself.

Chris Bonington
October 2001

PREFACE

"What can we gain by sailing to the moon if we are not able to cross the abyss that separates us from ourselves?" [1]

Our encounters with other people and the environment around us can be seen as our outer journey through life. A degree of uncertainty always attends it. There is another journey, however, that we all may take, which not only has uncertainty, but is also infinitely more mysterious. This is the journey into ourselves – the inner journey. Every experience we have of the external world has an effect, consciously or unconsciously, on our inner self. Through this process, we may come to understand that

What is within us, is without us
And what is without us, is within us [2]

* * * * *

To adventure in the outdoors can, and perhaps should, be a dangerous pastime. To a dispassionate observer, deliberately to choose to accept challenges that may pose a threat to existence might seem particularly pointless and difficult to justify. Yet for many, if not most, adventurers, the experience itself is sufficient justification to play on, or near, the very edge of safety. To perform well in situations exposed to risk, in places where the sensible might not dream of going, brings its own rewards. Initially, maybe, it is in terms of fun and enjoyment. Nearer that edge, these immediate feelings disappear, to be replaced by deeper feelings of elation and, in retrospect often, satisfaction.

As I have moved along this adventure-path of kaleidoscopic emotions, I have at first come to sense, and then to believe, that there is something beyond adventure. By saying this, I neither wish to denigrate nor to reduce the importance of adventure. To have an adventurous approach to life is vital for many reasons. What I am suggesting in this book is that the adventurer needs to have an open and attentive mind, and to reflect very carefully on his or her experiences. Once through the gateway of adventure, providing arrogance is left behind, there is a world of immense significance for those who travel there.

Although I began to adventure when young, I was too preoccupied with performance at that time to realise any deeper significance in these experiences. Then the wilderness took a hand and I never recovered. One particular experience in Alaska radically changed my attitude to life. I began to understand what it meant to feel oneself a part of Nature.* It also became increasingly clear to me, that the wilderness held a solution to the difficulties man finds in a world of his own making. Thoreau was surely right when he wrote, in the middle of the nineteenth century, "In wilderness lies the preservation of the world."[3]

I do not wish to take credit for the ideas I have put forward in this book concerning a possible framework of values for modern existence. These ideas might better be seen as part of a perennial wisdom. But I felt an urgent impulse to produce them in my own style. In doing so, I am conscious of two problems. The first of these relates to the subject. To consider values and the relationship between human beings and Nature is an immensely complex, often highly subjective, process. I am still in the process of attaining an understanding of the issues involved, and my own way ahead remains long. That is how it should be. Whatever my inadequacy, however, I have written to the best of my integrity. My respect and love of Nature would allow no other way.

The second problem is that I propose in this book a possible framework of significant values for human society, and suggest what seem to me key virtues. This can be seen as prescriptive or even grandiose, and is a most dangerous thing to do. It would have been much easier just to describe what I had encountered and deduced from my outdoor experiences, how those experiences had affected me, and left it at that. The reason I have taken the riskier option is simple. Whilst I completely accept that each human being must develop his or her own set of values, this is a lifelong search and "… at my back I oft times hear/ Time's wingéd chariot hurrying near".[4] Life is short, time presses each of us, and the sharing and recounting of experience widens our human perception. Even in my most optimistic moments, I fear that the leaders of the modern world are taking us, at an accelerating rate, down a destructive road. It is a juggernaut that stands in sore need of the brakes of contemplation and moral awareness that wilderness provides.

---

* Nature with a capital N is used throughout the book to mean the whole of the inter-related planetary system.

INTRODUCTION

Rock climbing and mountaineering; white-water canoeing and surfing; sea kayaking and small-boat offshore sailing – at different times, like attraction to a magnet, each of these activities dominated my life. Whilst each activity had its own specific and compelling attractions, in a sense they were all the same. They were all forms of physical exercise and adventure in the outdoors. Each could bring feelings of elation and success, a sense of awe at being in wild and imposing places, a sense of freedom and, occasionally, the fear of disaster.

Determined to perform at as high a level as possible, I committed myself to the demands of each activity in turn. Whilst I greatly enjoyed each of these environments, I was also driven by egotistical need for self-respect and the respect of others. I wanted to be a success, and was prepared to devote my energies to that end. Nature quickly taught me that the strength of a chain was in its weakest link and   I soon realised that there would be demands psychologically as well as physically. I had to learn to be relaxed in the inevitable moments of stress. I had to overcome fear in order to perform with maximum efficiency. I knew that I wanted to play on the frontier, near the edge of my capabilities, because that would bring the greatest reward. At the same time I knew that this frontier was often the thinnest of lines between triumph and disaster. There was at times an obvious need to be acutely safety-conscious if I wished to survive.

Whilst I was involved with, if not consumed by, these activities, I became increasingly aware that I had an intense curiosity about human existence. At university, for example, my enthusiasm was not for history as such, but for understanding gnomic statements such as Rousseau's, "Man was born free, and everywhere he is in chains"[5] or William James's, "The problem of man is to find a moral substitute for war."[6] Underlying this curiosity, I now suspect, was the search for an elusive state of happiness. I was by nature a less-than-content human being, and perhaps for that reason was attracted to dangerous activities. When I read *Markings* by Dag Hammarskjöld, within this riveting diary of a man under great stress from his post as Secretary to the United Nations, I found the following:

"The longest journey is the journey inwards."[7]

His use of the word 'journey' in the context of exploring and understanding one's inner self was like finding a diamond. I knew my own adventures affected me inwardly and, in particular, affected what I valued in life and what seemed really worthwhile about my existence. Nevertheless, my inner self seemed somehow separate from my outer actions. Henceforth, I began to see the whole of my life, both inwards and outwards, as a journey. I also began to understand that the inner journey was likely to be the most difficult and yet potentially the most rewarding. How far I could journey within myself would initially depend on the quality of my outer journeys – what I actually did with my life in terms of actions. It was much later that I realised the depth of the journey inwards would depend not just on the quality of my outward actions, but also on how deeply I could reflect upon them in terms of their value in understanding myself.

As I have become older I have come to realise that there is a wonderful mystery about being human, and about how we relate to our surroundings. Each of us is unique, and yet in many fundamental ways, we are the same. I have some insights gained from experience into this puzzle. Unfortunately, I sense also that any substantial and clear explanation is beyond words. But the attempt to express it I feel is worthwhile, in the hope that something I might put forward may be of help to others.

When we journey adventurously in the conventional sense – to climb a mountain or sail across an ocean for example – then the process is comparatively straightforward. The specific objective is decided upon and then the relevant skills and experience are developed and tested in the situation. If one wishes to journey inwards to begin to understand oneself, then the process is likely to be both confusing and complex. To me, it made sense not to try and confront directly this biggest of challenges. It seemed better to reflect first upon my outward actions, and also to try and learn from the experiences of other human beings.

Apart from an eventual desire to understand the values of my own adventures, my working life spent in Adventure Education seemed to demand that I should be able, as clearly and coherently as possible, to justify the use of dangerous activities as a form of learning. This was particularly pertinent after the massive publicity that followed the Cairngorm tragedy of November 1971 in which six young people died. This occurred on the Cairngorm plateau in appalling winter conditions under the aegis of a qualified instructor. Understandably there were shockwaves in the world of education, in Britain and beyond. Those in charge of adventure pursuits and young people were forced to reappriase their activities. Whatever the values of this type of education, I knew there existed the possibility of death or serious injury to someone for whom I was ultimately responsible. Being a Warden of an Outdoor Centre committed to adventure for boys and girls, that responsibility was made abundantly clear. The human being is fallible and there were some situations and conditions in the outdoors where the risk could not be justified for beginners.

In 1984, I wrote *The Adventure Alternative*.[8] It was an attempt both to clarify and emphasise some of the values that were in the great tradition of human endeavour in the wilderness. In retrospect, it now seems a blurred and unbalanced picture. I was too involved with adventure, and too enthusiastic about its strengths to see its potential weaknesses. I was also, at that time, only beginning to understand the extraordinary potential of what I would term the University of the Wilderness. I know now that it can provide the adventurer with glimpses of profound happiness, of joy, that are the stuff of dreams. *Beyond Adventure* is an attempt to redress that earlier imbalance.

CHAPTER 1

SELF

Myself, yourself, himself, herself

The German philosopher Schopenhauer wrote, "Know thyself and know the world".[9] My response to that remark, as a young man, would probably have been: "Of course I know myself and what is around me. I also, incidentally, know what I want from life and it is mainly concerned with the joy of climbing." Half a century later I wince at such an arrogant and ignorant attitude. Responding to Schopenhauer's maxim now, I would say, "I am beginning to know myself, but I accept it is a life-long process. It is an inner journey, and is primarily concerned with considered reflections upon my experiences of living."

It seems sensible to begin with the apparently simple, yet formidable, question of, "Who am I?" The initial answer might be that I am a whole person, a complete and indivisible form of life which remains a totality no matter what I do, and as long as I remain alive. Such a view I do not find immediately helpful. I need first to discern, if I can, the key aspects of what makes me human. As well as going into the outdoors, I need to go into myself.

* * * * *

Autumn 1961. I am a committed rock climber. The first teaching post I have accepted is at a residential school with a large new gymnasium. As a teacher of PE, I have control of this resource and I cover its brick walls with innumerable tiny wood blocks – possibly the first climbing wall in the UK. With little money, no vehicle and no local climbing friends, I devote as much time as possible using the gymnasium to train for climbing. An entire winter is spent in this manner and I can see marked improvements in physical strength and endurance.

Spring comes and it is back to north Wales for the first weekend climbing trip of the year. Tents up and, as the weather is fine, we head for an evening climb on Dinas Cromlech. I feel strong but not confident, as I have been away from rock for six months. I am drawn to a route called 'The Thing'. Although short, it has the reputation of being the hardest climb in the Llanberis Pass. (The contemporary guidebook description has passed into legend: "125 feet. Exceptionally severe. Extremely strenuous. A short vicious climb of great technical difficulty. Possibly the hardest problem in the valley. Difficulty is sustained, protection poor, retreat beyond the crux uninviting and the ground below nasty to land on.")[10] Halfway up the crucial first pitch, beyond the worst of the difficulties, I smile broadly. I feel no tension. Instead I feel immense physical power and my fingers seem like claws of steel. I complete the climb without difficulty.

Reflection: Physical strength, power and skill have always been important to me. To express this in the world of the vertical was to delight in being physically alive. It was a conscious delight in my own physical capability, more than in the medium through which it found expression.

* * * * *

Summer 1995. Day 87 of a trekking expedition. Annette, my wife, joined me on day 67 and together we are moving south through the Maritime Alps.

I have completed my aim of 1000 miles on this trip, but feel very low. In the debilitating heat, which even has the locals complaining, reaching the col above me seems to take forever. I collapse on the top of it and rest uncomfortably for an hour. Feeling a little better, I continue across the mountain and down to the next tiny village. Unbeknown to me, Annette has taken some of my gear, as she is worried about my condition. After a welcome coffee in the tiny bar and a long drink of water at the village font, we continue in the evening sun up the side of a gorge. I begin to slow again with a throbbing pain deep inside, and eventually stop. After discussion, Annette goes on, to find a suitable place to camp. About an hour later she returns. I feel no better and she takes my sac. By this stage I realise my strength is ebbing. It seems to take an enormous effort to put one foot in front of the other. Strangely, the only technical difficulty, a single log bridge over a drop into a rocky gorge of white water and menacing rocks, I manage without too much thought, unaware that it was the scene of a recent, serious accident. The adrenalin must have taken over. Once the tent is up, I try, without success, to find a position to relieve the pain. Discussion follows but there is only one sensible decision. Annette disappears back down the track to go for help. I remain in the tent and the eventual darkness, a prisoner of my gloomy thoughts. As someone who had worked for years on mountain rescue, I was now the victim in need of them.

Reflection: An overwhelming sense of physical discomfort dominated my pessimistic mood during this time and the subsequent hours of stretcher rescue, ambulance ride to Nice and first night in hospital. The pain was not sharp but throbbingly persistent and I could find no relief. Physically, I felt at the bottom of the pit. Illness was not something with which I was very familiar and the effects were devastating.

Both this and the previous climbing example were similar in that the physical nature, the body, tended to overshadow all other aspects of being human. It would be incomplete to leave it at that, however, because emotions were also deeply involved. The one event provided joy, whilst the other provided misery; but I will return to the matter of emotions later. I want to move on now to another key aspect of being human.

* * * * *

Summer 1976. Six of us are tackling the first circumnavigation of the Outer Hebrides by kayak. We have completed about half the 300-mile expedition and are having lunch at Vatersay before we head west, through the Sound of Vatersay, to the outer Atlantic coast. Despite the fine weather, there is tension. We sense the seriousness of the next stage and take particular care to check boats, gear and lifejackets. The large swell from the west breaks suddenly over the many reefs that litter the western entrance to the Sound. As we paddle, we take great care to avoid them. To be caught on a reef would be highly dangerous. Fortunately, the breaking waves indicate their submerged presence and we can take safe avoiding action. After several miles, and with relief, we are out of the Sound, beyond the reefs and in the deep water of the Atlantic.

The relief is very short-lived. The large ocean swell, on which we sit, moves calmly until it reaches the coastline. Then, with a thunderous roar, it explodes on the beaches to both north and south. It is immediately evident that to try landing on these beaches would be a desperate and foolhardy venture. Despite our surfing experience we have no wish to play this game. One alternative would be to return the way we have come, back into the Sound. We are even less keen on this option. The explosions of white water on the reefs we had previously passed held an obvious message: "Don't even think about returning this way." Going with the waves would give no prior warning of the reef locations, unlike our outward journey, where each one could be seen well beforehand. The option of rescue is also dismissed as unlikely. Whilst we carry flares, this coastline is uninhabited, and there has been no evidence of other boats.

The weather remains fine, but the exposure of our situation is considerable. There has to be some answer to our dilemma, apart from the unattractive possibility of rafting up overnight and waiting for the swell to decline. In theory the solution is simple. I have to find somewhere we can land out of the swell. Study of the map on my deck reveals one possibility taking into account the angle of the swell and the nature of the coastline. This is the tiny bay of Ardvuran round Greian Head about 10 miles to the north. Hours later we reach the bay and manage to land. As I walk up the smallest of beaches I realise that despite my love of the sea, I am a land animal.

Reflection: Standing out, like a beacon of light amidst the physical action, the kaleidoscope of emotion and the drama of the environment, was the study of the map to find a solution. In that short space of time I felt as though the whole of me was focused into that map. I had to find the answer. My thinking, the rational aspect of my brain, totally dominated.

* * * * *

Summer 1995. In the Pyrenees on a long trek with Annette. The previous day we had climbed a major peak by a trackless route, and were now on a minor track across lower mountains to a distant village for supplies.

The weather is sunny with a sea of cloud beneath us. As we rest briefly in a tiny wood, the weather suddenly changes. The cloud rises and a mist envelops us. Strong winds and driving rain follow. Our track, so clear on the map, is not to be found on the ground. To reach habitation involves a steep descent of at least 1000 metres of hillside. Many cliffs are marked on the map. For the next few hours I play a serious game of orienteering, except caution replaces speed and there is constant checking of our precise location.

Reflection: Once again, thinking out the problem to find the solution, the rational aspect of my brain took control of my being.

* * * * *

Up to this point I have put forward two key aspects of being human. The physical and the mental, and have given examples of when they dominated an experience. There is another key aspect, already mentioned, which is very complex and can be incredibly powerful. This is the emotional.

Summer 1963. The Romsdal valley, central Norway. There is no hint of what was to become the oddest climbing day of my life. Two of us, Pete Hutchinson and I, are seeking a training climb before we look at the unclimbed Trolltind wall. On the other side of the valley from the latter lay Mongeura, whose 1000-metre rocky face swept down into Romsdal. We could see from the road a natural diagonal line trending up right above much steeper rock. With the thrill of a new route looming, we set off with light hearts, a minimum of gear, and without food or drink. It is only a training climb and appears to have none of the aura of the vertical face of the Trolltind. The climb proceeds smoothly and enjoyably at about very severe standard, although we note that we need extra care with the rock and belays. We realise we are following a basaltic trap dyke where loose rock is common. At perhaps 700 or 800 metres above the start, the trap dyke peters out. A bulging corner of about 10 metres is the only obvious line. Immediately beneath the small stance is an overhanging void, the ground hundreds of metres below. Its impact is daunting, reminding us that climbing can be a serious game.

For about two hours I toy with the pitch above. Although short and not vertical, it appears holdless and there is no scope for running belays. I cannot see beyond the pitch although I sense it may become easier. Unable to forget the void below, I eventually and very reluctantly decide we have to retreat. This prospect is very worrying. With one rope and a few pegs and slings, we have to retreat safely, diagonally, back down the loose fault line we had easily ascended. With infinite caution, using the single rope both for awkward abseiling and protection, we finally reach terra firma. Retreat has taken eighteen hours.

Reflection: It was the only time in climbing that I experienced a strong feeling of success at reaching the foot of a climb. The predominant memory was of the underlying emotion of fear. Whilst it did not emerge in the form of panic, it pervaded me beneath the surface. Nature had been kind in this particular lesson.

* * * * *

Winter 1966. The Woodlands Outdoor Centre, south Wales. Mike Couch, Lindsay Williams and Ian Harvey arrive for a day's canoeing. They are experienced white-water paddlers and there have been days of torrential rain. The decision is taken to tackle the white-water-race section of the River Usk, below Brecon. The start indicates a flood level of about two metres above normal. I follow them down the river. At the top of the first big obstacle, known as Sphuler's Folly, I capsize and just manage to roll back up in the stopper wave below. A roller-coaster ride follows with what seems like giant standing waves and much confused water. There are capsizes in the group, but I manage to stay upright. We arrive safely at the finish. I express no desire to repeat the experience.

Reflection: From the moment my friends arrived at the Centre, and (I would assume) unbeknown to them, fear had lurked just beneath my surface. They were not only excellent paddlers but were highly adventurous. My fear was on two fronts. I had no wish to drown and neither did I want my friends to know that I was a coward. At the start of the trip the rushing brown water had filled me with gloom. My fears had surfaced at the top of the first fall, where I had tensed up and capsized. The emotion of fear had dominated me, a feeling perhaps that is part of the experience of any adventurer. What was fascinating psychologically was that as I rolled up from the capsize, the fear had been completely swept away. I was no longer tense, and was even able to enjoy the more difficult water below. By the time I had reached the end, my emotion had swung from the depths of fear to feelings of elation. "Wow, brilliant, great!" expressed how I felt. I knew, however, that I had been up to the edge of my adventure frontier.

Looking at the two experiences, they were both similar and different in psychological terms. In common was the end feeling of elation. In common, also, was the deep emotion of fear. It suffused my being. In the climbing it remained beneath the surface, whilst in the canoeing it surfaced dramatically. In both experiences the emotions at times held sway over the rest of my being.

* * * * *

There is a fourth key aspect of being human. This is the fascinating area, the proper domain of moral philosophy, which considers good and bad qualities, virtues and vices. We are, each one of us, a mixture of both. Those qualities or traits that we individually demonstrate in our actions, along with the motivation for them, seem largely to determine our specific characters. They also determine to a considerable extent our socially perceived quality as human beings.

1965–1971. Warden of an LEA Outdoor Centre, south Wales, for the City of Oxford. With an excellent team, I develop the Centre into a thriving and popular adventure base for young people. Annette and I begin a family. I find time for my own new adventures – sea-cliff climbing, surfing, sea kayaking and catamaran sailing – and write the first guide to rock climbing in Pembrokeshire. I also make time to write on adventure, to lecture on the subject, and to organise meetings that lead to the founding of the National Association of Outdoor Education (NAOE).

Reflection: This was probably the busiest and most hectic part of my life. Whilst physical, mental and emotional involvement in what I was doing were major aspects, the dominant factor was the quality of enthusiasm. Somehow I found the energy because I had total belief in the value of what I was doing. In particular I was deeply impressed by the virtues the youngsters displayed when faced with the often considerable challenges on the adventure courses. I became determined to do what I could to ensure that as many young people as possible in the UK had the opportunity of adventure as part of their education. They inspired me, and gave an insight into the positive potential of being human, which is so often undeveloped.

* * * * *

*1968. **Abseiling session**.* The Woodlands Outdoor Centre, south Wales. A group of ten 14-year-olds and two instructors. A 10-metre slab and safety rope with no danger involved. Nine of the ten complete the exercise with various degrees of psychological difficulty. Stepping over the edge at the top, even over a short slab, can be challenging. One overweight and poorly co-ordinated girl refuses to have a go. I send the rest of the group and fellow instructor off to another venue. I eventually get the girl on the edge at the top but she refuses to descend. I coerce her down by going down with her. She then goes down again, without me but with the safety rope. After several repetitions, she finally abseils down without the safety rope – something the others did not do. We rejoin the rest of the group. She is in a very happy mood for the rest of the day.

Reflection: There may, no doubt, be readers who will react to this experience along the lines of, "How dare you force a young person to do something against their will? You have no right. Such an action is completely unacceptable." Let me first put the experience in context.

It was, as far as I can remember, one of only two occasions where I acted in so an extreme a manner in the six years I was at the Centre. It is worth examining the event in detail. In essence, it was a battle of wills. She was determined not to do the abseil, but her decision was based on no experience of the activity. I was determined that she would do it. My motivation was solely concerned with the belief that she would benefit from the experience. In the event, she moved from displaying considerable determination – to the point of stubbornness – not to do something, to displaying the positive quality of self-confidence based on her own experience. Her final unprotected abseil demonstrated the key virtue of self-reliance. From being 'the one who failed in the eyes of the rest of the group', she moved to 'the one who had achieved the most'.

You may go on to ask, "But how did you know you would succeed with her, and what if you had failed?" There was no way, of course, that I could be certain of the outcome, but I had a strong intuition that it would be a success. This type of confrontation is one that most teachers will face at some time in their careers. I had a lot of experience, not only with young people, but also in situations where I was forced to do things that really frightened me. If I had not succeeded in this instance, I would have made a point of finding activities and situations where she would have been able to prove to herself that she could overcome her doubts and fears. I would not have left her defeated by them.

Central to this experience is the issue of the quality of determination, whether it is displayed as a negative, in terms of stubbornness, or in its more positive sense, as a virtue.

To summarise, there are key aspects within the complex whole of a person:

- a physical aspect

- a mental aspect

- an emotional aspect

- the qualities (the virtues and vices).

At different times and in different situations, any one of these aspects may dominate.

I have used my own experiences to illustrate these ideas because anything else is vicarious, or at a remove. We can be deeply inspired by the experiences of others, but they can never be as meaningful as our own. I would hope that the reader will be able to identify these key aspects of their own 'being', from their own experiences.

CHAPTER 2

DEEPER INTO SELF

Most of my younger life can be expressed in terms of mental, physical and emotional experience. It was often a bewildering mixture of all these aspects. My actions, too, or most of them, can be defined in terms of the virtues or vices I brought to each situation. What I was unaware of, as a young man, were two other aspects of self that were of immense significance.

Autumn 1957. At my parents' home. I have just returned from leading a university climbing expedition in Arctic Norway and am waiting to return to my studies at Oxford. The BBC news is on the radio as I have lunch. Vague interest becomes acute as a tragedy in the Himalayas is announced. I am devastated. My closest friend and climbing partner Bernard Jillot and another friend have been killed on the peak of Haramosh.

Reflection: As someone who did not make close friends easily, and whose relationship with Bernard could not have been stronger, my emotions searched my whole being. My world seemed, for a long time, to have little significance.

* * * * *

Spring 1958. At home in Derby. I am waiting to go climbing in Scotland. For something to do and with little enthusiasm, I go to a local tennis club dance. I am drawn to a young woman who seems to me the prettiest, and who is later to become my wife. I walk home in a daze, humming 'Some Enchanted Evening …'.

Reflection: To be in love is to experience a magic that engulfs your whole being and transforms even your perception of the external world.

Love and death – these two extremes of emotional experience – only now begin to fit into place. It is as though I am on the first rungs of a seemingly endless ladder towards deeper understanding. My belief now is that within each of us, whether we are aware of it or not, lies a centre. It is a profound and mysterious area beyond rational explanation. The best term I can find to describe it is the spiritual centre, but other words are also used: heart, soul, conscience, moral being, wisdom. I thought at first that it was the basic aspect of being human. Now I am convinced that it is the most important aspect of being human. I find it amusing and ironic – a neat paradox – that in these times where an attitude prevails of "if you cannot measure it, then it has no value", this essence of being human cannot be physically found.

But what is the importance of this spiritual centre?

I would suggest that it is the basis of what we value and the home of religious beliefs. It exists beyond our physical, mental and emotional aspects of character, all of which merge into it and emanate from it. It is the bedrock of our individual existence, which in itself is linked, in an even deeper, symbiotic sense, to everything around us. It is the basis of our sanity or insanity, and all points in between. It is the home of our dreams and nightmares, through which our subliminal responses to the external world are processed.

What concerns me is that the stress and pace, and the acquisitive frenzy of modern materialistic living can easily make us unaware that we even have a spiritual centre. Life is often too hectic in terms of making a living, having a good time, getting what we want or simply struggling to exist. As a result there is a spiritual vacuum in the man-made world, at least for the many who are not committed to religious beliefs. In the original plans for 2000 years of human celebration within the Millennium Dome, there were none for a spiritual zone, which illustrates the point.

To establish contact with one's spiritual centre can be extremely diffi- cult. Knowledge of its existence is one thing; feeling the certainty of its existence is quite different. Certainly for myself, and I suspect this may be normal, I was awakened to my spirituality only by reflection upon some very intense experiences.

In a broader context, I found the reaction to the tragic death of Princess Diana an event of considerable significance. It seemed to demonstrate the importance of the desire to praise and worship and connect. Millions of people were affected and moved by her death. Just for once the spiritual vacuum was filled, albeit in a sad and perhaps trivialised manner. I am aware that this massive reaction by the public could be seen as emotional mass hysteria, rather than as a spiritual response to a tragedy. That powerful emotions were involved cannot be doubted, but I sense a deeper significance. Those emotions, I feel, emanate from the spiritual centre. As I watched the funeral on television, tears began to well. I was not expecting to react in this manner.

* * * * *

The last key aspect of self I want to examine does not have the resonance created by the spiritual centre, but in its own way seems just as difficult to understand.

Spring 1981. The phone rings. Would I give a lecture on adventure and modern society? I agree and put the phone down. I feel great, at least until I realise that the lecture had better be good. The call is from Brisbane, Australia.

Reflection: I must be an important person. That was my view at the time, and for a long time afterwards. I now not only dismiss that view of myself, but regard my original view as a barrier to understanding myself. Viewing myself as important, I can now see, prevented me from beginning to discover who I am and how I relate to my surroundings.

* * * * *

1979. I am invited to lecture on 'Young people in the hills' at the annual BMC festival at Buxton. The event is primarily concerned with a celebration of mountaineering. Famous climbers are giving lectures. My lecture is 'odd man out' as there is concern in the UK climbing world about young people and 'education' appearing on the crags. I prepare very carefully as the subject is contentious. The lecture prior to mine, a visual show of two Americans soloing The Naked Edge in Colorado, is both wordless and stunning. I stand up in front of about 700 climbers with an utter sense of hopelessness. The audience's bent is towards sensation, and not consideration. I know I have failed before I begin to speak. I soldier on, wishing I was somewhere else.

Reflection: Although, in the event, it was not a disaster, I felt threatened by the powerful, if largely unspoken, view that the crags were only for the climbers and their perceived values. Psychologically, I retreated into my shell, sensing that whatever I said would be likely to bounce off closed minds. The previous film had emphasised the great adventure and solipsistic joy of climbing, and to the audience that was all that really mattered. I still felt I was an important person in my outdoor education world, but felt hurt and disregarded by my fellow climbers.

In both these examples, two lectures with very different audience reactions, I am referring to the ego. As I understand it, this is either a crucial part of conscious self, or simply is conscious self. It is that key aspect of being human which overtly encompasses the physical, mental and emotional sides, and individual qualities. It emphasises uniqueness. I can put it another way by saying that "I am enclosed in myself and everything else is outside of me" or "the ego is my separateness from everything around me". The lecture in Australia fed my ego and made me feel more important. The Buxton lecture diminished my ego. It made me feel less important because I could not make an impressive impact on the audience.

In my earlier days I don't think I was very aware of this basic aspect of being human, and certainly not of its dangers. I was too consumed with the brilliance of adventure and a life of action. If someone, however, had said I was egotistical, or self-centred to an extreme degree, I would reluctantly have had to concur. I would also probably have tried to defend myself by saying that single-mindedness in the pursuit of success at whatever I was doing was necessary. I might also have added that I was normal in having such an approach. Success and achievement are, after all, traditional and culturally approved aims in life. For example, at that time I had an E-type Jaguar. One day, driving up the M6, I kept my foot down on the accelerator until I reached 150 miles per hour. Speed then seemed to be meaningful. As I passed the traffic on the inside lanes, which seemed to be crawling, I was no doubt thinking, at least subconsciously, "I am an important person in one of the best cars in the world and this is what life is all about." At other times, as I crawled through small towns and villages and watched the envious glances from onlookers, when I looked down at that enormously long bonnet, similar thoughts must have passed through my mind. Years later I read something, which jolted me because of its truth – that a man's ego is in direct proportion to the length of the bonnet of his car.

I can now see that the ego can be so dominant as to become personal enemy number one. By this I mean self-centredness can be so extreme as to block out or prevent any journey deep into oneself. If the spiritual centre is the most important aspect of being human, then access to it can be denied by the barrier of the inflated ego. With any idea of self-importance is likely to come the vice of arrogance. This vice is characteristic of the modern world, and can grow at an alarming rate. Even – or perhaps, especially – heads of state, prime ministers, and other important people have succumbed to this state of being. There are recurrent examples of where the populace has become so sick of the arrogant attitude of their leaders that they have forced them off their pedestals. The opposite of the vice of arrogance is the virtue of humility. It can lead directly into the spiritual nature of being human, and is therefore of crucial importance. There is a paradoxical wisdom here. "The more successful we are, and the greater our achievements, the more essential it is to possess the virtue of humility."

I am aware that my analysis of self in these first two chapters is simplistic. In most situations in life any aspect of being human is not isolated, but merges or confuses into a personality which is itself subject to change. From what I have learnt it would seem that we should accept that *all* these aspects are not only important but are never static. They may grow and expand or diminish and atrophy. There is always a choice in this matter and it would seem obvious to go for all that is positive in the senses of being human. There is even a positive side to the ego. The latter may well be essential in order to find self-respect, confidence and affirmation, but it should never be allowed to dominate.

Another wisdom would seem to follow from the previous one concerning humility. How much we grow will depend not only on the quality of our experiences, but will depend also on the quality of our reflections upon those experiences. In other words actions alone, no matter how impressive, are insufficient. We need always to return to our base of values, our spiritual centre, in order to examine carefully how worthwhile are our actions.

To end the chapter I want to delve a little further into the mystery and paradox that although each of us is unique, separate, and different from others and from the world around us, in other senses we are all the same.

We are all the same in the sense that we have the same basic aspects of being human. (Including many I have not mentioned, such as instincts, drives and a subconscious.) We all come into the world through an essentially natural process and depart in similar manner – we are all part of Nature. Conventional living seems to indicate the opposite, in the sense that we usually feel separate from, rather than a part of, everything around us. We are deracinated rather than integrated in our world. This problem is explored later.

Despite the infinite variety of what we do with our lives, we would appear to have a common goal. Virtually all of us seek happiness and well-being. The search for these states, unless we are exceptionally fortunate, is likely to be lifelong and tortuous. That is probably in the nature of all human existence, and means, if we face up to it as best we can, that we are truly alive and on an adventurous and meaningful journey. The problem is, the journey in question has two apparently opposing directions – into the world outside and into the centre of ourselves. Somehow these two paths have the potential to meet in the form of well-being and happiness.

The fact that we are basically the same is a message of tremendous hope for the human race. Individually, however, we are each faced not only with 'sameness' but also with 'difference'. Because each of us is unique, distinctiveness and separateness are implied and often accepted as fact. It is a major intention of this book to try to question this common feeling, because separateness can, and does, easily lead to divisiveness, exclusivity and an unhappy world. As one thinks of 'separateness' and 'uniqueness' it may be important to remember that this is not specific to the human race. It is true of everything in Nature. Each flower, each leaf and each snowflake, for example, is unique and yet remains part of Nature. This should give us not only a sense of wonder, but also might suggest to us that there are deeper implications in terms of our relationship with the natural world.

CHAPTER 3

THE IMPACT OF OTHER PEOPLE

As a young man, my sense of personal freedom derived from engaging in those activities that I considered to be worthwhile. I tended to dislike constraints of any kind. 'A self-centred rebel' would probably be an apt description of me at the time that I was a student. There was certainly little thought or reflection beyond immediate reaction to events. Life was action and that, wherever and whenever possible, was the end of the matter. If anyone had mentioned moral or spiritual values, or ideas of an 'inner journey', I think I would have closed my mind immediately. When I reflect now on that period, I can see that the qualities of some of the people I encountered had a considerable impact on shaping my life. Consciously or unconsciously those contacts affected my values and, in particular, emphasised some of what I came to perceive as key virtues.

As an enthusiast for climbing, the inspirational figures from the sport's history became my heroes. I would frequent the libraries and head for the adventure section. Nearly fifty years later, I still do the same thing, although my adventure interest is broader now. In those days, my fervour was for the great climbers. The initial inspiration from Colin Kirkus and Bill Murray was expanded through the gripping exploits of the great alpinists: Bonatti, Harrer, Gervasutti, Buhl, Mummery and many others. Their accounts of derring-do in the high mountains I found both exhilarating and frightening. Climbing at this time seemed the greatest of life's games. I wanted to be a very good climber.

Fortune smiled on me. Oxford, like Cambridge, had a proud climbing tradition. Among the fellow students was Bernard Jillott, whom I mentioned in the last chapter. In one sense we could not have been more different. He was naturally charming, good-looking and on a scholarship to a top college. I was ill at ease in the rarefied atmosphere of Oxford, both socially and academically, and knew I had been fortunate to gain entry there. What drew Bernard and myself together was a passion for climbing. We both accepted without question that climbing was far more important than anything else.

This friendship grew in strength as we spent an increasing amount of time away from Oxford on the crags of England and Wales. Friction was conspicuously absent and I began to experience the pleasure of an extraordinary relationship. I could see the wisdom of Emerson's famous remark, that the most important thing in life is to have a friend. With such a friend I felt that eventually I could face the big climbing challenges. What made the climbing so enjoyable was not just the shared enthusiasm but that we were of similar ability. I was, perhaps, naturally more dynamic, but I could not match his unrelenting determination. A day at the Avon Gorge is an example. When trying to do a new route on the right side of the main buttress, he fell about 20 metres from the second pitch. After swinging on the end of the rope, he slowly climbed back up again. The second attempt again ended in a fall. By this time it had started to rain heavily and I presumed we would retreat. Limestone and water make an unfriendly combination on a bare steep wall. To my astonishment he insisted on a third attempt and only a subsequent repeat failure seemed to allow him reluctantly to agree to retreat.

His death in the Himalayas was a deep shock. The full story was told to me by one of the survivors – an epic that seemed to be on the same horrific scale as some of the worst tragedies on the North Face of the Eiger.[11] My anguish increased, and I was so dispirited I decided to give up climbing. Not for the first time in my life, however, the obvious decision was the wrong one. By good fortune, my college warden was the Reverend Eric Abbott, who later became the Dean of Westminster Abbey. He took me aside and, with great kindness, berated me for my decision. I left the meeting in no doubt as to my error. Bernard surely would have wanted me to climb even harder. I changed my decision and will never forget the manner of my mentor. His humility and incisive wisdom left an indelible mark.

Although to this day I deeply miss Bernard, I greatly valued some of my subsequent relationships with other climbers. Their positive characteristics left impressions which often inspired me in later life, when faced with other challenges. Some of them are permanently engrained in my memory. It is as though they exist vividly somewhere within me. Pre-eminent among these friends were Don Whillans and Wilfrid Noyce. Markedly different in terms of personalities and backgrounds, they were both outstanding mountaineers. For me, they were also heroes. Don seemed to be the less complex of the two. My friendship with him grew in an unexpected way. We had a row about the choice of route up a glacier on the approach to Trivor in the Karakoram. I realised that I had earned his respect by standing up for my viewpoint, even though I was very inexperienced. I also came to realise, later on that expedition, that I was prepared to follow him anywhere in big mountains. Allied to his skills, experience and exceptional physical strength were a sense of humour, immense determination and a fund of common sense. He was not a 'death or glory' climber, but rather a professional craftsman who had served a long apprenticeship. At home I could enjoy his company in the pub and occasionally beat him at darts, but could not compete in the drinking stakes. His approach to life seemed to have both balance and simplicity, and appealed in many ways. The fact that he was also egocentric and could be violent gave me little cause for concern.

If anything, Wilf was even more of a personal hero. Writer, poet and teacher, he was a remarkable man with a deep love of mountains. He seemed the epitome of the classical mountaineer. One unforgettable incident occurred when we were high on the Grade VI Welzenbach Route, on the north face of the Dent d'Herens. The route had not been climbed that summer as it was in dangerous condition because of a lack of good snow on the upper face. Once over the terrace in the centre of this face we became committed – with minimal hope of any protection – on steep, ice-glazed scree above an abyss. Wilf insisted we rope up. In effect, this meant that a slip by any one of the three in the party would certainly have led to tragedy for all of us. It was an action of extreme unselfishness and typical of the man. He had rejected the advice of the hut custodian in deciding to try the climb and took full responsibility for the fact that I was an alpine novice.

As memorable as this single action, and even more impressive, was his quiet, self-effacing manner. He seemed to exemplify the virtue of humility. There was never a hint of that arrogance which is so characteristic of successful people. I found this trait the more astounding when I considered his achievements on Everest and elsewhere.

During this period of my life I was essentially concerned with personal achievement through climbing. I find no pleasure now in looking back at this extreme self-centredness. Paradoxically, it was in trying to raise finance for the expedition with Don and Wilf to the Karakoram that I started to experience the pleasure of helping other people by sharing my enthusiasm for adventure. I had taken a temporary job as a teacher at a secondary modern school in the back streets of a Midlands town. My sole aim was to make money. I was convinced that I was far too selfish to be a teacher. It was as a climber that I planned my PE lessons, to train for climbing! Equipment was ruthlessly deployed to create challenging and continuous journeys that began at the door of the gymnasium and ended high in the loft above. To my surprise, the youngsters loved the sessions and even enjoyed my history lessons on polar exploration.

The experience of that term was the beginning of sharing my love of climbing with young people. It was also an excellent introduction to the instinctive needs of young people for adventure. I was so enthused by some of these youngsters that I took them climbing on rock. Two of them, and a particular day on Castle Rock of Triermain in the Lake District, I remember with particular clarity. Impressed by the ease with which they had followed me up Extremely Severe climbs, I pointed out to them the Very Severe 'Via Media' route and suggested they tried it. I went down to the campsite to make tea. They soon returned, smiling happily, unaware of the significance of doing such a climb. They had been without adults, were only fourteen years old and were in shoes. I later came to realise that this was an example of the potential of young people, given opportunity and careful, progressive training. It was also an example of genuine self-reliance at work in discovering one's capabilities.

My experiences at that school had, unexpectedly, led me to my vocation. It was to take a lifetime of work in education to realise the futility of trying to bring adventure outdoors into the curriculum in any significant way.* In those early days, however, my enthusiasm for adventure for young people burned brightly. That youngsters shared this enthusiasm was also evident in my second teaching post, at Manchester Grammar School. The idea of a schoolboy expedition to a comparatively remote wilderness quickly became a reality. In 1965, a party of 30 schoolboys and undergraduates left for an area of Arctic Norway. I had deliberately kept the number of adults to a minimum: a doctor, my wife and myself. Although I kept my thoughts private, I was determined to find out the capabilities of young people in an area wilder and more remote than any found in the British Isles in summer.

I need not have feared. Despite much bad weather, the young students,

---

* I was by no means alone in this respect. The late Lord Hunt, for example, was similarly frustrated. Even from his position in society, he failed to stop the wholesale destruction of self-reliant adventure for young people as part of their education.

working in groups of four on three-day expeditions from base camp, eventually climbed all the peaks within 100 square miles. The party then divided and engaged in activities ranging from botanical collections and glaciological surveys to exploratory rock climbing and first descents of white-water rivers by kayak. Over two months, there were inevitably many adventures, but accidents were few and minor. I returned to England more than ever convinced about the vitality, determination and teamwork capabilities of the younger generation.

These important aspects of being human had been severely tested in remote locations and yet enjoyment, satisfaction and fun had also been characteristics of that venture. That expedition was to prove an invaluable stepping stone to my next post as Warden of 'The Woodlands', the City of Oxford's new outdoor centre in Glasbury-on-Wye, south Wales. This was a deliberate decision to be, to some extent, unselfish. The pursuit of personal adventure as the dominant factor in my life no longer seemed acceptable. I wanted to try to make a contribution to society through education. There was no doubt that I enjoyed teaching adventure activities and there was always the additional attraction of being outdoors.

Initial pessimism about an apparently unexciting area on the River Wye, along with my then conviction that only some boys, and even fewer girls, of the 13- or 14-year-old age group would be adventurous, was soon dispelled. The next six years of responsibility for what was in effect a type of Outward Bound School was a very satisfying and educative process for me as well as for the youngsters. Almost all of them were complete beginners as far as adventure activities were concerned. They came from every secondary school in the city and were extremely diverse. Fortunately, they tended to display considerably more virtues than vices. They thrived on adventure, and they thrived also in the friendly yet purposeful atmosphere of the Centre. Their vitality and determination was often matched by teamwork and concern for the less able members of the group.

If anything their self-discipline, and particularly the control of their own fears, was even more impressive. A typical day in winter, kayaking down the River Wye from Builth Wells to Glasbury, may serve as an illustration. An all-day journey down this river, often in bad weather, would see frequent capsizes on the bigger rapids. Yet it was normal, after capsizing, for the majority to request if they could "have another go". To these beginners, one rapid in particular at Llanstephan, known as 'Hell Hole', when in spate must have sounded like the Niagara Falls. Somehow they controlled their fears despite shivering with cold (they had no wet suits!). At the end of these trips, they would frequently be unable to tie the kayaks onto the trailer, as their hands were too numb. Yet these youngsters would still be able to joke and laugh about their discomforts. Whatever was wrong with society, I felt sure these citizens of the future had the potential to shape a better world.

There were other significant messages from the 'Woodlands' experience. Whilst I greatly enjoyed being the Warden, despite the responsibility, I soon realised the importance of working with a good team. I was fortunate in this respect. The instructors were experts in, and enthusiasts for, their particular adventure activities. They were all strong characters – an essential quality for any good teacher – and they all genuinely cared about the youngsters. They knew their job was to try to provide adventure in safety, throughout the year and almost regardless of conditions. There were also local people who had the essential job of servicing the Centre. They were no less impressive than the instructors, and I realised once again that I was fortunate. Friendliness, open-mindedness, a commitment to hard work and an ability to face problems with equanimity reminded me that the yeomen and yeo-women of England were very much alive. There was a feeling of unity amongst the staff. They were doing something very worthwhile for young people and there was a justifiable pride in being committed to something exciting and dynamic. Of course there were frictions and the inevitable problems of high-pressure involvement in a small establishment, but the Centre usually had a warm and happy atmosphere. Many of the young people treated it like home, returning time and again.

It seems pertinent to comment briefly on the outdoor aspect of life at the Centre. To adventure for oneself is easy in comparison to being responsible for young people in what were, at times, dangerous situations. Considerable freedom was given to the instructors to decide both the locations for, and the nature and level of, the adventures. Constant vigilance in the outdoors was essential in such dynamic environments and yet in the first few years of the life of the Centre there were no safety regulations. Levels of adventure were often high, but in the six years there were no serious accidents. Responsibility, creativity, and a good relationship with their groups were characteristics of these staff. They had my trust, respect and admiration. As I was an instructor, as well as Warden, I knew the demands involved.

Trying to summarise how the 'Woodlands' experience helped me to shape my values I do not find easy. I certainly felt very privileged to have been involved in what was virtually a six-year-long social experiment. Once the officers of the Education Authority were convinced that we knew what we were doing and found that the young people were enthusiastic, we had their full support and were free to design the programmes.*

The most outstanding feature for me was the gradual realisation that young people had an instinct for adventure. In other words every boy and girl needed challenge in the outdoors and thrived on it. In later years I found no reason to change my views. Whole classes of primary school-children would respond in the same way.

Oddly enough, my belief in the importance of adventure for every young person also blinded me. I failed, then, to see that even adventure has a downside and can lead to arrogance and self-centredness. The reason I could not see this negative aspect was because I was too self-centred at that time. At 'The Woodlands', however, many of the virtues came shining through and strongly reinforced my faith in human nature.

This phase of my life was shared by my wife, Annette. Perhaps because I am opposite in terms of personality, I have always deeply admired her natural happiness and spontaneity, keen intelligence, creativity and unselfishness. Her combination of virtues have seemed to me rare in one human being, and have greatly helped me on my 'inner' journey. I feel a profound gratitude in my good fortune at having had such a life-companion.

'The Woodlands' also coincided with our having a family. From a very early age our three daughters, Vember, Senja and Tiree, would accompany us on expeditions to the islands of Scotland and the mountains of the Pyrenees. Even when very young, they were given small rucksacks and were expected to carry much of their own equipment. The challenges involved, in what were often long and hard days, were shared by the whole family. I still find it amazing that after such days these youngsters would go and play energetic and creative games outside the tent, regardless of the weather. These ventures were both excellent for forging strong family relationships and developing my awareness of key virtues.

As our children grew into their teens and beyond, I was able to observe the effect of outdoor experiences upon them and their friends over many

---

* Surveys showed that over 95% wanted to return to the Centre to carry on some form of adventure activity.

years. In 1971, I had moved from 'The Woodlands' to train teachers in adventure activities at Charlotte Mason College in the Lake District. As Ambleside was at the heart of a natural adventure playground, it seemed obvious to try and establish a community project through which local people of all ages could be introduced to adventure activities. The Ambleside & Area Adventure Association, known as 'The 4 A's', was created. The idea proved popular and was made possible by local experts in the activities, experienced outdoor students and a diverse range of local people. They all gave freely of their time and the project grew apace. In its heyday, fifteen different courses were on offer each term, and participants ranged from young families to senior citizens. Whilst there were problems that are perhaps common to all voluntary work, I could see the potential of any community working and playing together. All those involved could benefit in a variety of ways. Success in such a project was dependent particularly upon unselfishness. It was clear why this trait needed to be regarded as a major virtue.

Within the extensive programme, which operated mainly at introductory levels, there were also advanced courses for white-water kayaking. Over the years, I was able to witness startling progress by some of the young boys and girls. Despite the lack of good local white water, and the small size of the community, six of them eventually represented Great Britain in slalom and white-water racing. A number of the girls also went on to win international championships. What I found was unexpected. Whilst their levels of skill, fitness and determination were impressive, it was their attitude to competition that was striking. On being asked, for example, what were their priorities for a forthcoming competition, they replied as follows. "Firstly, we want to have an enjoyable time and secondly, we hope someone in the group does well." I found this a refreshing contrast to the conventional attitude of so many competitors, who are determined to win at all costs and who can be extremely selfish and aggressive because this is deemed essential for success. These young people were teaching me a fundamental wisdom. Enjoyment, satisfaction, and even perhaps happiness can be found through a very strong friendship group that is not primarily motivated by personal success. In a sense of course they were an example of the old adage that 'it is the effort that counts, and not the result'. Once again I realised the importance of humility as a virtue. I was supposed to be teaching them, when, in a deeper sense, I was the learner.

Just as impressive was the fact that this group, along with similar groups of 11- to12-year-olds, underlined to me the importance of another virtue, that of self-reliance. Over a period of years, groups of up to 10 youngsters completed five-day expeditions in the hills and down rivers, without adults. Whilst the responsibilities were considerable, everyone involved, including the parents, were deeply impressed by the effect of these journeys on them. There was no doubt that even young people of this age, carefully trained, were extremely capable of being self-reliant. They also gained considerably in terms of self-respect, self-confidence and in how to work efficiently with each other. Put in perspective, they were completing the equivalent of the Duke of Edinburgh Award gold expedition two or three years before they could even have joined that scheme!

Looking back, there has been a pattern to my learning from other human beings. Friendships had a huge influence, especially in my younger days. My vocation meant a very fortunate mix of adventure and the outdoors with school children of both sexes and of all ages. This was then balanced, later in life, by working with students and teachers, which, together with the community work, involved the entire age range. Throughout this time, there was also the crucially educative process of marriage and bringing up of a family.

In the most basic terms, I had moved from taking what I wanted from life to sharing my enthusiasm for adventure and the outdoors, and then to giving substantially to others. In that process, other people have helped me to grow, to respect key virtues and to move closer to developing a framework of significant values.

CHAPTER 4

THE IMPACT OF NATURE

In this chapter I want to concentrate on how the natural environment affected me up to the time I became involved in sea kayaking. This youthful period covered 16 years of commitment to climbing, followed by several years of white-water kayaking and then open-boat offshore sailing.

Prior to all these activities, however, I enjoyed six months of exploring the underwater world. It was to be an experience that had an unusual message, which I only appreciated much later in life. At the age of 20, in my final months of National Service, I was posted from northern England to Brighton. The posting displeased me because I could not have been further away from rock climbing. By good fortune, on the other hand, I was put in charge of sports equipment and given money to spend. There was only one available solution for an adventurer. I bought masks and flippers. It seems almost unbelievable now, but each morning I would leave the barracks to walk down to the sea and test the equipment. I was always alone, as other soldiers preferred the bright lights of the town.

My new adventure proved anything but boring. As confidence and skill grew, I would increase my distance offshore and the depths to which I dived. Whilst there were no coral reefs or sharks, there was something else that I unexpectedly enjoyed. Beneath the turbulence of wind and wave lay a world that was pristine and peaceful. Alone beneath the waves I was to find harmony.

There was also, in contrast, the dynamic world on the surface. Going out in strong winds and big seas was exciting. The flippers gave me great confidence and, as each wave roared down upon me, I would dive beneath it. This process continued until I was well offshore. I would then dive to the seabed and find quietness. One bad weather day was especially memorable. As I surfaced from the seabed and began to return to shore, the buildings on the seafront disappeared from view for long periods. The impressive waves rolled past me to smash on the shoreline. When I finally landed, somewhat thankfully, about a mile down the beach from where I had set off, I realised I had been lucky. It made total sense when, years later, I read in the introduction to a classic book on ocean sailing, that the first quality necessary for any seafarer was humility.[12]

After National Service, I went up to Oxford and back to the world of climbing. Climbing tradition at Oxford inevitably led to plans for visits to the big mountains. An expedition to Arctic Norway was followed by my first visit to the Alps. This proved to be a highly memorable yet somewhat depressing experience. On my first route, an 'extremement difficile' (ED) on the East Face of the Grand Capucin, I was sufficiently in awe of the scale of my surroundings to let my partner, Pete Hutchinson, a fellow student at Oxford, lead the climb. Whether it was because Pete had previous alpine experience or simply more determination, or both, I soon realised I did not possess his impressive self-confidence. Ironically I did not find the actual climbing too demanding. Both on the tricky descent from this route, however, and a retreat from above 'the fissure Brown' on the West Face of the Blatiere in a storm, the dangers and complexities of descent seemed frightening.

As arranged, I left Pete in Chamonix and took the train to Zermatt to climb with Wilfrid Noyce and Jack Sadler, an American. The three of us were to use the experience as preparation for an expedition to the Karakoram Himalayas the following year. Our first climb reinforced my doubts as to whether I could enjoy big mountains. With only two days of snow and ice experience on Ben Nevis, I found myself on the Welzenbach route (ED), on the North Face of the Dent d'Herens. After the unusual experience of breakfast at midnight, we set off from the hut. Traversing unroped on an easy, but narrow, snow ledge above a 200-metre steep face on the lower section of the mountain, I inadvertently tripped over my crampon. As I hurtled down the slope, with a yawning bergschund far below, I knew I had to learn the skill of braking with an ice axe. I eventually stopped myself about halfway down the slope, climbed back up, now very awake, and rejoined the team. I had been lucky. Only fools learn basic skills in such dangerous places.*

Below the upper main face, a short overhanging bulge of snow and ice posed an entry problem to the face. Wilf and Jack decided it was not possible, and we were faced with either retreat or a very lengthy and problematical

---

* This occurred below the roped-up section mentioned in the previous chapter.

traverse. I could see, however, that I might be able to use artificial rock climbing techniques to overcome the bulging wall. Using the ice axes and some long pegs I was soon over the problem. It felt good to be a useful member of the team. The main wall above, however, proved extremely scary as it could not be protected, and it was with considerable relief that we reached the top unscathed.

Our next climb, the Lagarde-Devies route on the Macugnaga face of Monte Rosa, did nothing to improve my enjoyment of snow and ice. It seemed obvious to me why this Grade VI climb was unpopular. After two days, on what was one of the biggest faces in the Alps, my abiding memory was of considerable avalanche risk, with debris everywhere on the lower slopes and complex route finding. There was little technical difficulty.

I was relieved when Wilf agreed that my last climb should be back on rock. When I had arrived in Zermatt, Paul Biener, a local guide and a friend of Wilf's, had suggested we tried the Furggen Ridge of the Matterhorn. This was the most difficult of the Matterhorn ridges, with the Direct Finish graded VI, and it had not had a British ascent. As I had been overwhelmed by my first view of this magnificent mountain towering over Zermatt, I was completely enthusiastic. After a bivouac by the rubbish dump outside the overcrowded Hornli hut, Wilf led the way to the base of the ridge. Disappointment at the ease of climbing and the poor quality of the ridge at first dampened my enthusiasm, but at least I was to lead a whole climb. On the high shoulder, where the normal route left the ridge, was the Direct Finish. My enthusiasm returned as I led up good rock, at about Very Severe grade, and soon reached the top.

Enjoyment of the spectacular view from the uncrowded summit was short-lived. A severe snowstorm swept in. As I followed Wilf down the Hornli ridge it became obvious that there were many climbing parties having problems coping with the conditions. I knew I was fortunate to have such an experienced mountaineer as my guide. His judgement of where to descend in the blizzard conditions and his confident movement over all manner of terrain were inspirational and reassuring. The midnight meal in Zermatt, that night, rounded off what had been a magnificent mountain day for both of us.

That first alpine season was a seminal experience. Any sense of achieve-ment at doing difficult climbs and first British ascents was counterbalanced by the knowledge that I was ill at ease in dangerous mountain environments.

I had ignored the matter of progression – that most basic message of all from Nature – at least in terms of being and feeling competent in such places. There are some very fortunate people who can psychologically make the leap from very small to very large dangerous environments with equanimity. I was not one of them. I needed carefully and progressively to gain confidence in my surroundings before I took on the bigger challenges. Only in this way would my psyche allow me to perform with the relaxed concentration so essential for overcoming difficulties and feeling contentment in the process. That simple yet fundamental message had been basic to my rock-climbing career, as I had worked my way up through the climbing grades in Britain. How stupid and how arrogant it now seems to have jumped immediately into difficult alpine routes. The fact that I coped well with the climbing itself could not hide my feelings of vulnerability in large mountains. Some years later, after doing a new route, in error, in the Brenta Dolomites, I found I was thinking the unthinkable – of giving up serious climbing. I knew that my rock climbing in Britain had reached a plateau, in the sense that I could not see my skills improving much further. I also knew that, despite being attracted to the big mountains, I would only find the relaxed concentration I felt I intuitively needed if I could spend frequent amounts of time in their midst. This seemed impractical. Sadly and despondently, I decided that I would no longer allow climbing to dominate my life.

Something to replace climbing seemed essential, and I chose kayaking because I remembered enjoying canoe journeys as a schoolboy. Enthusiasm developed rapidly when I discovered that white-water kayaking was as adventurous as climbing. In some ways it seemed even more so. There was no rope for protection and fast water was a much more dynamic environment than rock. I spent some years learning the basic skills, being fortunate enough to be taught by experts from Manchester Canoe Club. At one stage, I was tempted to commit myself to slalom competition. In some ways it was a very attractive sport, being exciting and yet essentially safe. Being informed, also, that I might make the British team was tempting as well as being good for my ego. I soon tired, however, of weekend competitions where most of the time was spent off the water and success was measured on the contrived and very short route of a man-made course. Whilst it could be exciting and was excellent for the development of boat-handling skills, it singularly lacked the adventurous feelings of a wilderness journey. The alternative was simple. I would work my way through the white-water grades in the British guidebook to the relevant rivers. Progressive experience, as with climbing, led to increasing competence, and I was able to enjoy paddling Grade III and Grade IV rivers. It seemed sensible to avoid the two final grades of V and VI, especially as the latter carried the warning "cannot be attempted without risk to life".[13]

A few hours one winter's day was sufficient to impress upon me the immense power of nature. Exploring new rivers had become a passion. Careful study of map contours revealed that many rivers fell steeply in upland areas. Whilst for most of the year such rivers were too shallow to kayak, there were distinct possibilities in winter after prolonged rain. The River Vyrnwy in central Wales looked particularly interesting. One weekend, after a fortnight of almost continuous rain, it became the destination. My wife was to drive, and my companion on the water was Stephen Schaeffer, Head Boy at Manchester Grammar School, where I taught. He was very fit and adventurous, but comparatively inexperienced. As we drove towards the head of the river, we were surprised to see a minibus and canoe trailer pass us, going the other way. We were later to discover that these were experienced members of Birmingham Canoe Club who, on careful inspection, had decided it was suicidal!

The start, a mass of swiftly moving brown water, was impressive but canoeable. This took us down to a sharp bend, and the roar of water beyond indicated caution. We went ashore and had to climb in order to see what lay ahead. Thirty metres or so below, the river went through a gorge. Although the river was moving very fast, there were no visible rocks. Somewhat quietly we returned to our boats. There seemed no logical reason not to continue. Once round the bend, we were immediately committed to the gorge. We had completely failed to realise that our high view directly down onto the river gave no information as to the size of the waves and the complexities of breaking water. Thoughts of Grade VI flashed through my head to be instantly dismissed by the need to concentrate. We were in a maelstrom of surging brown water of a size well beyond my experience. At first this natural dipper ride was immensely exciting as I managed to keep the boat upright. Just as I was thinking we could cope, however, I saw ahead a swollen side-stream powering into the main river. I knew I would have to do a strong recovery stroke as it hit the boat. The problem was unavoidable. Despite forewarning, I had no chance and capsized. I had to roll, which I managed with difficulty. The drama was just beginning. As I spluttered upright, very relieved, I saw Stephen suffer the same fate. He failed to roll and my entire energy was then committed to his rescue. It was probably another quarter of a mile before I could get to the bank, with Stephen hanging onto my boat. We finally recovered his boat in trees about a mile further down.

Maybe luck played a considerable part on that day. Further experiences on flooded rivers seemed to pose a similar dilemma to that which I had found in climbing. If I wanted the exhilaration and feelings of power brought by playing these games somewhere on the edge of my capabilities, then I had to accept the possibility of the gravest of consequences. The attraction of 'the edge' was very strong, but I think what turned me away from it – at least in terms of extreme levels – was that in the final analysis I did not have complete control of what happened. No matter what level of skill I reached, and no matter how hard I worked to find that 'relaxed concentration', there would always be an element beyond my control. It seemed highly possible, and even logical, that the more one played on this dangerous frontier, the more likely that the inevitable would eventually happen.

My white-water kayaking subsequently tended to stay below Grade V and took an unusual direction. It is taken for granted that rivers are kayaked downstream. Working on the River Wye from 'The Woodlands' Centre, I began to seek an alternative. I would try to paddle up the river from Glasbury-on-Wye to Builth Wells. This eighteen-mile section is generally Grade II, with one Grade III rapid. Going against the current would present a very different challenge. I would have to kayak up the Grade III rapid 'Hell Hole' when the river was in spate. It was not possible in normal river levels. A river in spate, however, meant considerably more current going against me for the whole trip.

Obsessed by the idea, I decided when I was physically ready and waited for the right river level. It proved a fascinating journey. The final rapid at Builth Wells is inconsequential when going down river. Going upstream, it presents a strong current for almost half a mile with minimal resting places. I knew that by the time I reached the foot of this final section, I would already be extremely tired. From the outset, therefore, my aim was to go up each rapid with the minimum expenditure of energy and to be as rhythmic and skilful as possible.

You may be wondering what this experience has to do with the impact of nature on me. The answer is an important one in terms of how, much later in life, I came to understand more of my relationship to nature. This uphill journey may well have been highly unusual in the human world. In the world of the salmon it was normal. I was doing what they did. At the foot of every rapid I would rest in the eddy and then use all my power and skill to move efficiently upstream. Thinking like a salmon was my attitude to this type of kayaking. I had nothing but admiration for this magnificent fish. I could also begin to understand what they must have felt like when they reached their journey's end. I had only travelled eighteen miles and yet my back muscles were so seized up that I had to lie flat for some considerable time before I recovered. The salmon, on the other hand, may well have travelled from Greenland. Such thoughts at that time were probably another reason why, years later, I did not like the idea of fishing, even in a remote wilderness.

Whilst at 'The Woodlands', the pressure of work and its effect on family life led to buying a house in Pembrokeshire. From high mountains and white-water rivers, my enthusiasm for adventure now moved increasingly towards the sea and its wild coastlines. I became entranced with both environments: so much to enjoy and so many places to explore. A decision to try sailing was made. Initial arrogant impressions that it was not very adventurous were soon dismissed. A friend, for whom I occasionally crewed in local evening sailing races, lent me his Osprey dinghy on a windy day. With another inexperienced friend, and only a basic knowledge of the theory of sailing between us, we were soon immersed in water. When upright, however, there was no doubt that this was an exciting style of journey. I wrote to a famous sailing journalist, explained my background, and asked for advice on what type of boat I should buy. His reply was brilliant. I could either be conventional and purchase a second-hand Wayfarer dinghy or opt for an unconventional open racing catamaran. As a lover of speed, especially fast cars, there was no choice.

The 'Unicorn' was built by Sam Cook, a fellow instructor, and myself over a winter at 'The Woodlands'. It emerged as a boat of considerable beauty. Twin hulls of about five and a half metres in length with a maximum of a less than 20 centimetres width in their central section, a trampoline deck, trapeze and an alloy mast with a single 14 square metres (150 square feet) of sail seemed to breathe speed. With three-millimetre-thick marine plywood hulls and weighing less than a hundredweight, it was designed for Olympic-class single-handed racing in sheltered waters.

Once built, the next stage of learning how to sail the boat was often hilarious. On the small local lake, instant and impressive acceleration up to speeds of over 20 knots was often matched by 'diving'. The cat would bury its bows up to the base of the mast and the crew would disappear underwater on the trapeze. At other times the boat would flip completely and much time was spent finding ways of re-righting it. In winter the sailing became unbelievably cold even without capsizing. No matter how much clothing was put on, the cold remained. Nature was teaching us the obvious lesson that if you are sitting on a wet platform in freezing wind, there is no way you can stay as warm as when working hard in an enclosed kayak. Cold, however, was often forgotten in the exhilaration of speed from this pure racing machine. As our skills developed we spent more time on the water than in it, and began to sail efficiently. We knew, however, that taking a lightweight racing thoroughbred offshore would require a very cautious approach.

For some years, with the onset of each summer, the catamaran would be taken down to Pembrokeshire. Weather forecasts were intensely studied for the arrival of high-pressure systems, and then the journeys were made. As with other types of adventure, an increase in skill and experience led to more distant horizons. Most journeys were memorable, and some felt very special. These included traverses of most of the Welsh coastline and a single-day, 100-mile journey across to Lundy, Devon and back to the Welsh coast. Eventually, after waiting almost a year for appropriate weather, the exposed 70-mile crossing from Fishguard to Rosslare in Ireland was also completed. On this journey, despite high-pressure weather, we almost looped the cat when far offshore. Within hours our arrival in Ireland was followed by an easterly gale.

Waiting for the weather was to be a major reason why I eventually gave up this activity. Whilst I agree with Emerson's statement that patience is one of the most important things Nature can teach man, in the case of catamaran sailing I am not so sure. To justify going on these adventurous journeys necessitated having high-pressure weather systems. British weather is notoriously fickle and such systems can often be a rarity. Even in these good-weather slots, these journeys could still be exposed and dangerous in such a tiny open boat. It also took time to realise that the thrill of this type of sailing had a marked downside. The stresses and strains on a catamaran, compared to a single-hull boat, are far greater. Added to this is the battering caused by larger waves offshore. The strength and quality of all the fittings thus became a crucial factor in terms of performance and safety. Preparing the boat for these journeys seemed like preparing a rally car to the last nut and bolt. This had to be done for each journey, as we were determined not only to be safe but also to be as professional as possible.

The final reason I gave up this special form of adventure was that it needed two people. As in any form of serious adventure, and possibly more so because of the tiny confines of shared existence, compatibility, as well as competence, was essential. My crews were excellent, but life moved on for all of us. It became really difficult to find a suitable crew.

It was hardly surprising, coming from a background of great enthusiasm for sport at school and for little else, that I should approach climbing, kayaking and sailing as simply bigger games. It was obvious that the bigger or more serious the game, then the greater the stakes. If it involved any danger to life, it was a higher form of game and would bring greater rewards in terms of feeling. I felt sure that these adventures were superior to more conventional sports, although the experts in games played on pitches and in sports halls with man-made rules in front of crowds would no doubt strongly disagree. My sympathies lay with Nietzche's famous saying, "Believe me! The secret of reaping the greatest fruitfulness and the greatest enjoyment from life is to live dangerously!"[14]

Despite success and enjoyment in the sports arena, I had no doubt that for me the wilderness environment was far more appealing. There were no rules apart from the unwritten message of "the strength of the chain is in its weakest link". Whilst bad weather and occasional deep fear were distinctly unpleasant, there was a delight in the freedom and beauty of the outdoors, and in being 'far from the madding crowd'. There were, however, no thoughts at this stage, of any 'inner journey' or of spiritual matters.

Life seemed essentially uncomplicated. I loved adventure and enjoyed the outdoors. When staff at 'The Woodlands' or students at Ambleside commented that I seemed different when I was out of doors with them rather than within the confines of the base, I used to smile. Of course I was different. Freed from all the constraints of the man-made world, its meetings, phone calls and endless paper, I was more alive. What I never went on to say was that I only felt fully alive when I was completely away from education in its entirety! This remark needs careful explanation.

I greatly enjoyed my work in Adventure Education at all age levels. I was also convinced that it had considerable value. Teaching relevant skills for adventure was always interesting, but my principal enthusiasm was for finding adventure situations. I strongly held the view that Nature was the real teacher, and that my role was that of facilitator. In other words, I wanted the learner to experience directly the impact of wilderness, with as little interference as possible from myself. My responsibility was to set up the experience, or opportunity, and to be as sure as possible that there was an efficient safety framework. That was largely how I had learnt, although often without the framework, and it seemed the right approach. I was only to realise the real significance of this approach, that of self-reliance, much later in life.

The disadvantage of such an approach was that it eventually required, when those being taught were basically competent, a high degree of responsibility. This was accepted, sometimes with considerable inner pressure, because it seemed the 'right thing to do'. I can see now that my love and respect for the natural environment would accept no other approach. This was also why I had little but contempt for those instructors and wardens of centres who polished their images in front of beginners but did not adventure seriously themselves. Such people seemed to deny the real potential of adventure for those in their care and to debase adventure itself. They are like the goal-scoring football master in the Ken Loach film 'Kes'.

Once I was completely away from the restraints and responsibilities of formal education, I had the freedom to face challenges commensurate with my own experience. I could live on my edge. In some ways this was a selfish attitude. I had considerable admiration for those who committed themselves almost totally to teaching. Extreme unselfishness has a great deal to commend it, but as an approach to life it seems unbalanced. In one sense I could see education as a form of escapism. There seemed to be some wisdom in the cliché "those who can, do; those who can't, teach". In saying that, I think I was regretting that I had not gone completely down my own road of adventure.

Returning to the matter of being fully alive in my own adventures, my experiences of different types of adventure in diverse environments held the same messages from Nature. If I was to go towards the edge in each one of them, I had to accept that this would require the best of my abilities and the maximum of effort. Because I loved adventure, the challenge was accepted, even if I knew there would be considerable ups and downs in the process. The demands on specific fitness, skills, mental co-ordination and emotional control in stress situations were all obvious requirements. Less obvious perhaps, but of no less importance, was the development of awareness of one's surroundings. One's survival at times depended upon this factor. I can now see that this awareness tended to be very narrow, focusing primarily on the immediate area of the environment with which one was involved, whether it was a piece of rock, or a rapid or complex sea waves. Whilst there was nothing wrong with this approach, I was eventually to realise its limitations.

This narrow focus was also present in my human relationships. I wanted to be recognised as an expert. It seemed logical to expect such recognition because of the effort and commitment required by each activity. Any adventurer is likely to recognise this conventional approach. Status and success seem acceptable goals, alongside the excitement, satisfaction and often elation basic to dangerous pursuits. If someone had come along at this stage in my life and had said "What about your ego?" I think I would have had to take time out to consider such an odd question. I might eventually have replied, "Yes, of course my ego, my conscious self, was very deeply involved. By definition adventure is self-centred. In other words adventure is egotistical. If I make a mess of a challenge, I might have a nasty accident. If I overcome the challenge, and especially if it is on the edge of my capabilities, then I deserve to feel great, and I will enjoy any status that comes my way. In other words, I am a normal human being."

If the same awkward person then went on to ask, "But what about the spiritual centre of being, which you now say is the most important aspect of being human?" I would have been unable constructively to reply at that time. If I had been compelled to a reply, it might have been something like, "The spiritual must be something to do with religions, and I have no interest in such affairs. I am a man of action." I would now answer that question very differently: "My deepest aspect, or the base of my values, was affected in these activities. I tended, however, neither to understand nor to appreciate their spiritual significance. I suspect they were stored in my subconscious, and only much later in life did I begin to understand their value."

If the wilderness could somehow have spoken to me after my pursuit of these activities at this stage in my life, it might have said this:

"I respect your efforts, commitment and enthusiasm for adventure in my natural world, but your ego is making you blind to who you really are. You must try even harder with your adventures, but try also to leave your ego behind. This has no place in the natural world of which you are a part. Because you are a man of action it is even more important that you reflect very carefully and with complete honesty on your experiences. Do not be fooled into thinking that your adventures alone will give the answers. Look at the whole time you spend in the wilderness. Pay attention to the world around you. If you do not, you will never discover who you are. Please have some reverence for these wild places. They are sacred."

I look back again and more broadly. Amidst the blur of many adventures, I have missed the matter of beauty. Certain distinct memories surface.

As a sixth-former I had illegally taken a day off school, hitched up to Derbyshire gritstone and climbed on Gardom's Edge until I ran out of energy. My enthusiasm was for the rhythm of climbing and the challenge of technical difficulties. There were no thoughts about the beauty of the place. Nature, however, seemed to have other plans. As I sat fatigued on a large prow of rock I became acutely aware of the magnificent sunset and how all the rock around me became suffused with its glow. In those moments I felt at peace with myself, and the world.

Years later, one September, I lay in my sleeping bag alone on a mountainside in Arctic Norway. It was the end of a climbing expedition and I was musing on the difficulties of a long hitchhike to Bergen with almost no money. Nature again took me outside of myself. Light started flickering in the sky and for the next hour or so I was treated to the magic show of the Northern Lights in all their glory. I was spellbound by the beauty of the shimmering curtains of different colours.

Very closely linked to the sense of wonder aroused by these experiences is what I would term a sense of awe. Again memories surface.

I was alone at a base camp in the Karakoram Himalayas. Don Whillans had gone down the valley to meet the main party. I lay on my mat, enjoying the sun and cloudless sky. Suddenly, I became aware of darkness. Opening my eyes, I saw an enormous eagle hovering directly above me, blocking out the sun. Momentary panic – I remained tense. I watched in fascination. Eventually the eagle soared away to glide for many miles down the valley. It flapped its wings once.

I sat on a ridge of rock that jutted out into St. Bride's Bay in Pembrokeshire. It was winter and I was perhaps 50 metres above the sea, and yet soaking wet from the spray. Discomfort was irrelevant as I watched the effect of a force nine gale on the ocean. I was transfixed by the power and majesty of the maelstrom beneath me. Words of a famous sea canoeist came into my head, "I can paddle the sea in a force ten." How ridiculous this comment sounded when applied here, and what nonsense the trait of arrogance it expressed.

A friend and I were offshore in a tiny open catamaran. We had left Pembrokeshire in the early hours before dawn and were heading for Lundy Island, 40 miles to the south. Wind and sea were slight, but the day was gloomily grey and we were silent. For many hours we had seen no sight of land, and I was unused to such a situation. Beneath the disquiet was a deeper feeling of awe. I was no more than a speck in the great scheme of things.

A group of us were watching the River Wye at Hell Hole rapid. It was our local river, on which we had canoed for years in all types of conditions. On this occasion we had left the kayaks at the Centre. The River Wye had become the first item on the national news. It had wreaked havoc in massive floods below Hereford. The power of this six-metre flood, within the confines of the steep-sided valley at this place, reduced us to quietness. There was no rapid here, only a succession of massive standing waves that every so often collapsed, only to re-form. Uprooted trees and wreckage appeared and disappeared down river.

In all these instances, the sense of awe and wonder, subconsciously, had affected the centre of my being and in some way or other had affected my attitude to life. It may well be, of course, that both senses are part of the same thing. They would appear to be inextricably linked to feelings of beauty. "Fair seed-time had my soul, fostered alike/ By beauty and by fear".[15]

What I have been trying to suggest is that the impact of Nature on those who adventure is potentially much more than the normal and somewhat obvious physical, mental and emotional involvement. In particular I am suggesting that those often fleeting, unpredictable moments of awe, wonder and beauty are possibly more important, because they directly involve the depths of being human. I suspect that one's ego and immediate physical, mental and emotional states are all suspended. In those precious moments there is a strong hint that there is something beyond adventure which is a joy to experience but seems beyond the reach of our understanding.

To complicate the picture further, I want to describe some other experiences, which at the time I did not understand.

In a remote mountain area in Arctic Norway, I led a friend up a new route, as part of a university expedition to a region where there had been no climbers and the choice of routes was endless. The enjoyable route, at about Hard Very Severe standard, changed character. I was faced with a much harder 30 metres of arête. Despite being by nature extremely cautious and very safety-conscious, I decided to commit myself to it. Although protection was poor, I somehow flowed up the pitch.

I was sailing the catamaran in Carmarthen Bay in south Wales. The wind was fairly strong, about force five or six, and I was on a 10-mile reach, the fastest point of sailing. Instead of taking the comparatively safe option of being well offshore, I deliberately sailed the boat along the irregular shore-breaking waves. There was now a double challenge of both sailing and surfing the boat at the same time. On what was a bright and beautiful day, the boat screamed along in white sheets of spray. Somehow this unseamanlike and somewhat silly challenge had become a magic carpet ride.

In both these and some other experiences, there were immediate reactions that they were 'great'. At the time, I was unaware of their real significance. It was to be sea canoeing that would lead me into some understanding of the more elemental messages from Nature.

Throughout the climbing, white-water canoeing and sailing phases of my life, I took it for granted that I was separate from both my surroundings and from my friends. Any suggestion that there might be a unity with anything outside of me I would have dismissed as ridiculous.

CHAPTER 5

SEA KAYAKING AND ALASKA

"To glimpse one's true nature is a kind of homegoing,
to a place east of the sun, west of the moon." [16]

In 1981 I set off on a solo sea kayak expedition up the coastline of
south-east Alaska. In the light of what proved to be the most profound
of all my experiences, and one which was to change radically my attitude to life, it seems important to relate some of the background relevant to
that journey. I can now see a range of factors that were a build-up to that
experience.

The initial attraction of the sea for me was its surf. The excitement of
riding the waves on a good surf beach became a passion as, coincidentally,
did the music of the Beach Boys. It was not just that 'Good Vibrations', for
example, was a magic track. There was also the basic message that there is
no substitute for hard work. Apparently it took them 90 hours to perfect
this piece of music. A house in Pembrokeshire meant both work and play
were possible in this dynamic environment. As with anything else in life,
enthusiasm and the time to live an activity soon led to skills and competence. Inevitably in the rougher conditions, and with the more advanced
techniques of looping and running the bigger waves, I capsized frequently.
Staying in the boat when upturned and then Eskimo rolling back up again
was to become second nature. It was to be a skill of vital importance when
I moved on to sea kayaking.

The time came when I felt a strong urge to explore beyond the surf line.
The Pembrokeshire coastline soon proved adventurous. Miles of sea cliffs
with few landings, tide-races and exposure to sudden weather changes
demanded that journeys be made with careful preparation. Playing in the
surf onto a particular beach was usually fun. Offshore, the game was much
more serious. Weather forecasts needed to be studied, as did tidal information. It also became essential to know the competence of each member of
the group. Whilst easy conditions might prevail for hours or even days,
serious situations could quickly become a reality.

When I moved to Ambleside, after some years committed to catamaran sailing, I returned to sea kayaking with renewed enthusiasm. The attraction was not so much the Cumbrian coastline but the islands of Scotland, which were now more accessible. Again I was fortunate to be able to spend a considerable amount of my work-time as well as recreation pursuing this enthusiasm. A glance at the map of Scotland will reveal a complexity of islands off both the north and west coasts. From spring to autumn over a period of years I began a project to see if I could canoe round all of them – in a not dissimilar way that some people become Munroists.

During this period I took time out to organise what was the first sea-kayak expedition from Britain, using a boat named the 'Nordkapp' that had been specially designed with bulkheads. The 1976 Nordkapp expedition was a six-man journey of 500 miles from the town of Bödo up the Norwegian coastline to the North Cape, the most northerly point of mainland Europe. It was to be an interesting journey, but was not as enjoyable as I had anticipated. Very bad weather prevailed for the first part of the journey, with snow down to sea level. The coastline often lacked excitement, and beaches were a rarity. On the other hand, not only did the weather and coastline improve markedly in the latter part of the journey, but throughout the trip the Norwegian press made us headline news. This meant, in effect, that when we reached any form of habitation we were treated with great hospitality. We returned pleased with our success. Much had been learnt about this type of extended expedition and the 'Nordkapp' was to become the most popular design of sea kayak, worldwide, in later years.

After this expedition I returned to the islands of Scotland with increased confidence. My next major challenge was an attempt at the first circumnavigation of the Outer Hebrides by kayak. Off Barra Head, the most southerly point, I was introduced to the difference between an oceanic swell and a sea swell. Despite fine weather, my companions disappeared from view for long periods, hidden by the glassy sea-swells beneath a 200-metre cliff. Talking to the lighthouse keeper afterwards, he assured us that fish had been found on top of these cliffs. We felt no inclination to disbelieve him. We were in awe of where we had been.

After that journey I continued to try to circumnavigate all the islands. As I did so, from the Inner Hebrides and across the Pentland Firth to the Orkneys, I enjoyed discovering the uniqueness of each island. I also found I was becoming more confident in sea kayaking on my own. There were occasions when canoeing partners were unavailable and my enthusiasm for this type of adventure would not allow me to stay at home. Whilst I missed the companionship, I did have complete freedom and was to find contentment in being alone. From a safety viewpoint, I knew that when conditions were dangerous almost certainly self-reliance would be the crucial factor. I was aware that in very rough conditions none of the canoe group rescue drills was likely to be effective.

I was eventually ready to face up to a local challenge that I had studiously avoided over many years. The Cumbrian coast did not have the attraction of Scotland, but it did have the Isle of Man offshore. In the right conditions, this island can be seen lying 40 miles away. On a fine day one July, and after very careful preparation of the boat and equipment, I drove to the tiny hamlet of Bootle on the coast just south of Ravenglass. Locals, enjoying the peaceful evening, helped me down to the sea and I paddled into a glorious sunset. Many hours later I was in darkness and could see no land. All I could see was a large bank of sea fog to the south and I was tense. There was still a long way to go and no way to know exactly what the complex tides were doing to my tiny craft. Suddenly a small bird fluttered around the boat. It stayed for several minutes and was obviously curious. My curiosity became excitement. It was a storm petrel, also known as a sea swallow, which is normally only ever seen well away from land. As my sea kayaking had developed so had my enthusiasm for sea birds and this was a special sighting. I paddled on and, to my relief, found I no longer felt tense. A little while later I saw a distant light on the Isle of Man and was able to adjust my course. Arriving on the island eight hours after the start, I was pleased with the adventure. I remained, however, very puzzled by the effect of the bird encounter. Something had happened in those moments that I would only begin to understand many years later.

Later that same year I decided on an expedition to Alaska and invited Barry Smith, who had been on the Outer Hebridean expedition and also to Cape Horn, to accompany me. Maps revealed a possible 700-mile journey on the Pacific Ocean from the town of Prince Rupert on the Canadian/Alaskan border northwards to Sitka, the old Russian capital of Alaska.

In a practical sense, like the Nordkapp expedition, this journey was a mixture of hard physical work and easier days; times to relax and times to come to terms with dangerous conditions. In a psychological sense the two expeditions were extremely different. Whilst there was considerable beauty to be appreciated in both environments, I was overwhelmed by the magnificence of the Alaskan seaboard. This was a world where immense environments come together. We paddled, as two specks on the edge of a great ocean, in an area of 16 million square miles of forest, with 5000-metre mountains beyond. Three other factors encouraged a sense of awe as we journeyed onwards. The sea teemed with life forms: fish beneath us, sea lions, otters and various types of whales, often close to the kayaks. Birds, too, were fascinating – brightly coloured ducks, loons with their hauntingly beautiful cries, bald eagles and ravens watching us from rocky promontories. Our fascination with all this natural life was enhanced by the lack of human presence (apart from our fragile intrusion). We were acutely conscious that we were in a majestic wilderness. Few, if any, people also presupposed another factor that made an indelible impression. There was virtually no pollution.* Coming from Europe, this was a delightful surprise, as even the remotest and least visited beaches and coves of north-west Scotland are often full of the foul debris of man. It was unsurprising, therefore, that I fell in love with those surroundings. I use that word deliberately because it is the exact word. And it seemed a small price to pay that the black bears on land were a potential hazard, and that we needed to be careful where we camped.

I decided that, if at all possible, I would return to Sitka, and therefore left my boat with the local undertaker who had become a great friend. Waiting around for a flight back to Anchorage, I checked out the local bookstore. Whether it was mere luck or serendipity, what I came across was fortuitous. I passed the long flight home engrossed in *The Wilderness World of John Muir*.[17] Quite apart from finding his writing on the wilderness inspiring, what he confirmed for me was the idea that I would make my next expedition a solo one. It seemed highly pertinent that not only had many of his adventures been solo, but that he had also been north of Sitka and had a glacier to his name, in Glacier Bay.**

Back home in the Lake District I realised that I must not underrate what I intended to do. A 700-mile journey up the outer coastline north from Sitka

---

* The 'Exxon Valdes', a few years later, was to spew her oil over this pristine coastline. I still shudder at the thought of the terrible devastation that was caused. It is almost as if I can feel the damage inflicted.

** In England at that time his writings were virtually unobtainable and his name largely unknown. It is pleasing to see that since then he has received considerable publicity.

towards Prince William Sound and Anchorage was an exposed venture. I obviously needed to be very kayak-fit. To that end, and because time was limited by the demands of work, I used Lake Windermere, close to my home, as a training ground. Over that entire winter I tried to paddle on the lake daily. Many of the sessions were at night. Conditions were often unfriendly and occasionally dangerous. I quickly came to respect this flat-water environment. I then realised, to my surprise, that my feelings were much deeper than that. I had come to love the lake in all its moods. I also began to hate all the pollution and speedboat activity on it that so violated its nature.

During the training a very odd event occurred, which I shall describe now, but will reflect upon in the next chapter. One afternoon, I was returning from a 10-mile training paddle in easy conditions on the north end of the lake. As usual, I was pleased to be in the boat, which I regarded almost as home, but I was very tired from my exertions. With about a mile to go, something happened which had never happened before despite thousands of miles of paddling. It was never to happen again. I suddenly flowed. Water, paddle and I merged. Movement felt completely effortless. As I came into shore, onlookers commented on my paddling. Somehow they had sensed that something special had occurred.

I was also concerned about other possible problems of a solo venture. In terms of safety I knew I had to rely essentially on my previous experience. Whilst the fishing boats had two-way radio communication and access to frequent, regular weather forecasts, this was not possible for me. There was simply no room for the necessary equipment in the restricted storage space of the kayak. In any event, I did not feel it appropriate to take such equipment. For the same reason I carried no gun. It seemed somehow wrong, even though the bear danger was a reality.

Another potential problem of being alone was the psychological one. I did not know if I could live with myself for a month. My longest previous solo journey had been for a few days and, as any solitary traveller knows, time is of a quite different dimension from shared living. It is, or seems to be, of much longer duration and feels much more intensive. Put crudely, a week can seem like a month, or even longer according to the nature of the experience and various other factors. It was obvious that this aspect might be a major challenge in addition to the practical challenges of the journey. All I could go on was that my previous solo experiences had not given me any undue problems, and I had valued them highly.

Before moving onto the journey itself, it seems worth emphasising the following.

- The kayak is a tiny open boat and, when heavily laden, is more in, than on, the water.

- Kayaking is essentially a silent mode of travel.

- I was completely comfortable in the boat. Years of experience meant it fitted like an old slipper and, if necessary, I could sit for over 12 hours without real discomfort.

- I was treating the expedition as another adventure challenge and was expecting both physical and psychological dangers. I felt I was ready to undertake the experience.

- Competitive feelings were irrelevant, as I was alone.

Over the previous few years I had increasingly become much more aware of, and enthusiastic about, the sea. I was in love with my chosen environment, that of the ocean.

Early on a morning in July 1981, I headed northwards in my kayak from Sitka. I arrived back just over a month later after a journey of around 650 miles. Although the original aim of reaching Prince William Sound had been abandoned because of prolonged bad weather on the Outer Coast and the preponderance of bears in that area,* I was more than content with a full exploration of Glacier Bay. Inevitably with a journey of this kind there were many memories of different adventures in a superb pristine environment. Of infinitely more significance than what I did was what happened to me psychologically. I would ask you to forgive me if I find difficulty in expressing what happened. My words are inadequate in this context. I am not referring here to the normal range of moods that reflect the wide variety of conditions on the journey, but something very much deeper. This is what happened.

After the first few days, I gradually became aware that, when on the ocean as distinct from on the land, I had the deepest feelings of contentment. To say this was odd would be a very considerable understatement. I am not by nature a happy and contented person, as friends well know. More than that, it was in my nature to be anxious and consequently tense whenever I was in

---

* The Rangers of the Glacier Bay station informed me that, on a visit by floatplane, they had not landed on the Outer Coast because of seven grizzlies on the shoreline.

situations where there was, or seemed to be, any sort of threat. This attitude had remained constant whether it was a social or adventurous situation. I lived with this tension reluctantly, because it seemed both a basic and irre-movable part of my personality. Yet here, this underlying tension had not only disappeared but had been replaced by opposite feelings of deep well-being. The best way I can find to describe it is as follows.

You are in a kayak on a journey along an exposed and wild coastline. Your boat has a keel only just beneath the surface, which means there is always a high possibility of a capsize. As you paddle along, the balance of you and your boat are strongly affected by the wide range of different sea conditions. You react accordingly in terms of practical actions, always trying to keep the boat upright. Then, somehow and inexplicably, your kayak is given a keel so deep that it has no base. You have become completely stable. This idea is, of course, practically ridiculous, but I am referring to your psychological state. In other words, beneath the wide range of moods and feelings as you journey along, there is now an underlying immense feeling of stability and contentment. Your kayak may still be basically unstable, but now you have complete psychological stability.

To experience this depth of well-being fleetingly would be a gift from the gods. What I still find amazing was that these feelings were present throughout the expedition whenever I was on the sea.

In contrast to this deep contentment offshore, I was distinctly uneasy for much of the time when on land. Unpleasant as this was, it was unavoid-able. Unlike the previous expedition to Alaska, this journey further north was in an environment where both black and brown bears were common. I had been told at Sitka that a solo kayaker had been killed by a black bear in Glacier Bay the previous year. This was apparently unusual and was much more typical of brown bears or grizzlies. Either way it was bad news for me, especially as I carried no gun.

Because the forest usually descended to near high-water levels, most of my camps were on the edge of, or just in, the forest. This meant that no matter how tired I was, sleep was difficult. The inevitable sounds in the forest around me at night brought disturbing thoughts of bears in the vicinity. My projected landings, once daily for lunch, were also often a time of frustration. On several occasions lunch was taken in the boat with a bear watching me from my chosen beach.

The obvious point to make here would be that the danger on the land resulted in the good feelings offshore. I feel confident that this deduction is wrong. There were certainly feelings of relief, sometimes very strong feelings, when I left the land each morning. The immense feelings of contentment on the sea, however, were much deeper than mere relief.

The climax to the last full day of the journey illustrates this. After the peaceful grandeur of the Glacier Bay area, I headed westward, via the tideraces of Cross Sound towards the open and exposed Pacific Ocean. After a night at East Cove, a temporary base for small fishing boats, I left very early the next morning. Out of the lee of the land, I ran into a big swell, a keen northerly breeze and thick sea mist. The atmosphere was gloomy and frightening. Using a compass I worked my way south-west, sheltering when possible in the lee of small islands. Staying close to land proved difficult because of massive beds of kelp, but eventually the mist lifted and my route became clear. The sun now also shone and lifted my spirits. Unfortunately the wind began to increase and I could see an ominous front of bad weather coming in from the West. By the time I reached the end of Lismore Strait and was out in the ocean, it was becoming dark, was pouring with rain and the wind was strong. I can distinctly remember thinking, "What an incredibly stupid place to be on a Saturday night!" It was only a fleeting thought, as I was in a dangerous situation. Capsize was a distinct possibility in rough seas breaking on reefs. I had to make a decision either to go south towards Sulphur Bay, where I knew I might just be able to land, or to try and return into the comparative safety of Lismore Strait. As I tried to make this decision, in increasingly threatening circumstances, I realised, to my astonishment that it did not matter. What I mean by that, I hope I can explain. For the first time, in all my adventuring and the occasional situations where death had been a distinct possibility, I realised I now regarded that possibility as irrelevant. Instead of being extremely tense, which I expected when danger threatened, the inner depth of serenity was still present. I would use every ounce of energy, skill and experience to survive, but I was intrinsically happy to accept that these were surface reactions only. I could now accept the wisdom that the most important thing in life is to die at the right time. We all have to die sometime. When we depart, it is best that we are doing something we love.

Although it's irrelevant here, you may like to know what subsequently happened. I managed to retreat into the Strait, and after several miles arrived at a lone building that I had previously passed. In the dark and pouring rain I knocked on the door and asked for permission to put up the tent. A very shocked Alaskan stared at me, and I could see he was thinking something like, "Are you for real?" After a long pause he said, "Cabin and shower are over there; dinner in 20 minutes." Contrast in living could not have been more extreme or more enjoyable ... thick steaks, fresh vegetables, beer and a long night of 100% proof Yukon Jack whisky. At last I had found a deep sense of contentment on land! It was the perfect end to what had been a 55-mile day of fascinating kayaking.

I returned from Alaska in what was in some ways a confused psychological state. Something had happened that seemed inexplicable, but clearly said to me, "There is something in the wilderness that is both profound, and beyond adventure." I hoped that, eventually, I might begin to understand. Significantly, and unusually, on my return I had no wish to publicise any aspect of that expedition.

CHAPTER 6

ELEMENTAL EXPERIENCES

Experiences that transcend normal living

I t was to be many years before I began dimly to understand what had happened to me inwardly on that Alaskan journey. It was to take even longer to appreciate its vital significance. Initially, I puzzled as to why it had not occurred previously, and especially on the Alaskan expedition with Barry. The answer to that seemed comparatively simple. Barry and I were, and remain, friends, but there was an edge between us. In the presence of danger, my competitive nature inevitably produced a tense atmosphere when with other people. This was always likely to work against feelings of deep harmony with one's surroundings.

I have long accepted that the sea is alive. This is a sense common to many who have spent time on it, and especially, perhaps, for those in small boats and those who commit themselves to surfing. This did not, however, directly explain why I experienced such peace and harmony within. Even now I stand in awe of the unfathomable depth of that feeling. I came eventually to Jung's theory of the 'collective unconscious' and realised that in it might lie part of the answer.[18] In my travels in different parts of the world it had been notable how many outdoor enthusiasts had asked me if I had read Jung. His theory of the collective unconscious is, in essence, that the history of the human race and everything that affected it is imprinted in each of us. I take 'everything' here to mean 'everything in the natural environment'. So the natural environment was in some mysterious way imprinted within me. In Alaska, therefore, that part of me that was the ocean had somehow been switched on. I had experienced an 'oceanic feeling'.*

This particular Alaskan episode for me had been extraordinary, and completely unexpected. Until I'd lived through it, I was unaware that I could possess such feelings during an entire expedition. In trying to begin

---

* This phrase comes from Romain Rolland. Freud discusses it at the beginning of his classic essay 'Civilization and its Discontents' (1930), where he glosses it as "a feeling of an indissoluble bond, of being one with the external world as a whole".

to understand what had happened, I sensed intuitively that I had encountered something of the reality which is beyond rational understanding and for this reason beyond accurate verbal description. No wonder Aldous Huxley had written, "Sell your cleverness and buy bewilderment".[19] I had long been suspicious of cleverness. Far too often it was used for manipulative and egocentric reasons. Much more importantly, I now appreciated that cleverness was seldom useful in the search for wisdom. When I looked up the meaning of 'bewilderment', I was delighted. Not only did it mean mentally confused or confounded but it could also mean 'pathless', a word descriptive of wilderness. 'Bewilder' could be read as 'be wilder'.[20]

Reflecting further on the oceanic feeling, the implication was startling. Instead of accepting the fact that I was a part of nature, I now felt that, potentially, I was Nature. This idea initially disturbed me. Even to have the potential to be Nature seemed extremely arrogant. Then I recollected those occasions when I had felt no more significant than a speck of dust. It seemed eminently possible that we all have the capacity to feel we are nothing, everything, and all points in between.

The more I thought about this experience, the more important its message seemed to be. Indeed, I wonder whether this idea of unity with nature should not be regarded as the most powerful of all the forms of wisdom to be learned from the wilderness. I had journeyed through life for forty-seven years, accepting as fact that I was separate from both other human beings and the natural environment. My conscious self, my ego, did not question this. I accepted it as my normal, rational state, and as far as I knew, the same was true of everyone else. I now know that deep down I have a unity with Nature, because I have lived that unity.

Nevertheless, the idea that everything in Nature was within me as well as outside of me still seemed illogical, if not ridiculous. It was reassuring, therefore, to discover that there is a tradition of this wisdom handed down through the ages:

"What is without us is also within
What is within us is also without" [21] *(The Upanishads, 600 BC)*

"I and all things in the Universe are one" [22] *(Chuang-Tzu, 4 BC)*

"You never enjoy the world aright, till the Sea itself flows in your veins" [23] *(Thomas Traherne, 1674)*

"Every part of the universe contains the whole universe
enfolded within it" [24] *(David Bohm, 1983)*.

Even very recently, consider the Laplanders in Arctic Norway, who were
totally against a scheme for a hydro-electric dam, despite considerable material benefits because, "The river here is part of us".[25] The Lapps were
expressing a truth and a sacred sense of place that is characteristic of so
many people who have lived in harmony with the Earth. It is a voice that
has echoed down the centuries, repeated and emphasised by individuals
who have lived, worked or journeyed attentively and simply in their natural
surroundings.

So far I have been referring to one very unusual episode in my life. I
came to realise there were other personal experiences that had seemed
extraordinary, appeared inexplicable at the time, affected me deeply and
that might have something in common with the Alaskan journey.

The climb in Norway and the catamaran sailing in Carmarthen Bay
(described in the chapter on 'The Impact of Nature') had similar characteristics. They were both in dangerous situations and, unusually, I had
chosen the bold course of action. In the sailing I had taken the more difficult route through breaking seas close inshore. In the climbing I had decided
to tackle a pitch that normally I would have avoided. Neither decision
seemed particularly sensible or rational but the rewards were considerable.
I felt that I had 'flowed' up the climb and across the waves with a natural
skill that made light of difficulties, which normally would have taxed me
considerably. I can see now that in both those experiences I had subconsciously been at one with the environment – with the rock and the waves –
and this had expressed itself in exhilaration and elation.

This feeling was perhaps even more acute in the example mentioned in
the last chapter, when training in the kayak on Lake Windermere. Unlike
the previous examples, where both the exciting environments, possible
dangers and effects of adrenalin may well have given me a heightened sense
of awareness, Lake Windermere was very familiar and presented minimal
danger. Yet seemingly from nowhere I was to experience a period of effortless paddling that has remained unique in all my years of kayaking. For this
to occur on the flat water of my local lake rather than some wilderness
coastline seemed to make it even more unforgettable. Because I can
remember this occasion in some detail I will reflect further upon it.

The human being is a complex of billions of cells in interconnected systems. To have a situation where the whole of you is suddenly in complete harmony is likely to be magical. When you have spent years, for example, trying to perfect the skill of paddling which is in itself very complex, and you suddenly 'flow' effortlessly, it is as though you were projected instantly into another very elusive and wonderful world. What was especially significant was that it did not in any way feel restricted to a matter simply of physical involvement and technical skills or reduced to any of the scientific and psychochemical 'explanations' – of body chemistry, for example, concerning substances such as endorphins or decomposing adrenalin. I felt as though the whole of me, consciously and subconsciously, was merged into this experience. In that sense, I would say in those moments my entire being was in complete harmony. I had experienced a unity within myself. To ignore the lake, however, would be to miss something of even more importance. As I paddled through the water, for the final ten minutes or so, movement was effortless despite my being very tired. The word flow describes exactly how it felt. Logic dictates that to move a paddle through water, as with all physical actions, effort must be involved in order to make progress. Once again such experiences appear to defy the laws of science. 'Defy' is perhaps the wrong word in this context; 'are beyond' would perhaps be a better phrase. In any event, the key feature of this experience, as in all the others, was the feeling of oneness. In those precious moments, my separateness from the situation had vanished.

If all three of these events emphasised a bonding with my surroundings then it was in an immediate sense – with the water through which my kayak moved, the waves through which the catamaran sailed and surfed, and with the rock I climbed. A fourth adventure while sailing gave similar feelings but in a much broader sense.

Two of us were returning from Holyhead on Anglesey across Morecambe Bay to the Lake District in a small open catamaran.* By nightfall, and after about thirteen hours of slow sailing in light airs, we had reached the main channel into Liverpool. We were about ten miles offshore and, unbeknown to us, we were about to be given a considerable fright. (If we had known what we were getting into, we would have turned south-east from our northerly heading and waited on shore for daylight!) Night sailing

---

* A 'Shearwater': 5 metres long with 46 square metres of sail and the deck only about two-thirds of a metre above the sea. It is a boat capable of 20 knots, but very vulnerable and exposed in rough conditions.

was a new game for me, but for the next hour or so, instead of finding excitement, I found terror. Stupidly, neither of us had bothered to check the time of high water. It had seemed irrelevant when we knew we would be miles offshore. For the large boats that plied in and out of Liverpool, however, the time of high water was the critical element in determining when they arrived or departed from the city. By chance, high water was occurring as we started to cross the shipping lane. To make the situation even more interesting, it was not only dark but the wind had freshened from the east. Trying to decide which lights were moving and in what direction, and which lights were fixed, was a nightmare as we tried to cut across this busy marine motorway. In the situation, our single torch was obviously a joke. 'Small is beautiful' is an excellent maxim, but in this case it was more like 'small is lethal'. Hearts in mouths, we felt at one point we were doomed. A liner, or similar vessel, ablaze with lights, seemed to be bearing down on us, no matter which way we steered the boat. When we finally reached the deserted waters north of the shipping lane, we knew we had been extremely fortunate to escape.

My crew, Mike Waites, who had spent some years in the Merchant Navy and had shouldered the responsibility of reading all the lights in order to determine a safe course, retired to sleep on the trampoline deck. The next few hours until dawn were very special. At the other extreme of deep emotion, instead of suppressed panic I felt unbelievably happy. At first this did not make sense as I was very tired and the situation was still dangerous. The wind was now fresh offshore and the boat was moving fast through sheets of spray. A capsize would have brought severe problems and pushed us further out to sea. Yet the feelings of deep contentment could not be explained entirely by the relief at crossing the shipping lane. Somehow, almost in an ethereal way, as night in the outdoors has often seemed to have some magical quality, the fatigue and dangers appeared irrelevant amidst so much startling beauty. A huge moon in a starlit sky, the long ribbon of yellow light from the Lancashire coastline far away to the East, and the green phosphorescence from the spray and the wake of the rudders all combined to make the deepest and most indelible of impressions. Even now, it is as though it happened yesterday. At the time, I had no thoughts of the merging of man and nature. It was simply seen as an experience of extraordinary beauty and power. Now I realise that I must intuitively have felt an integral part of this magical scene.

Offshore at night in a tiny open boat would seem a likely environment for such feelings. Inside a lecture theatre might seem perhaps the least likely. During my lifetime I have given many lectures. Only once did I become aware of feeling awe. At the end of the slide-lecture, which, significantly maybe, was on the beauty and challenge of Nature, there was an unusual and profound silence. It was obvious that, as the lecture progressed, all of us had been engulfed in the same wave of deep emotion. In other words there had been a 'logic-defying' unity among a small group of individuals. I was later to come across accounts of similar feelings at large sporting and musical events.[26] It became clear to me that feelings of separateness in the human world could be transcended on any scale, bringing together in a total involvement the performers, performance, spectators or audience, and place.

There have been other personal experiences of this kind, more frequent although still rare. The strange meeting with the storm petrel on the kayak night crossing to the Isle of Man was a case in point. That meeting of a few minutes had a radical and highly beneficial effect on my mood. From the exhilaration of paddling into a sunset, I had become tense in the darkness. The threatening bank of sea fog to the south and no sign of any lights on my destination far ahead emphasised the gloom that I felt. I was intensely lonely. Somehow the storm petrel removed my gloom. I became confident and relaxed as I paddled onwards. During the encounter, feelings of loneliness gradually disappeared. It was like the unexpected arrival of a very close friend, only more powerful. In essence my feelings of separateness from my surroundings had somehow disappeared.

The raven is well known both for its intelligence and its ability to play.[27] Among the native peoples of North America, it was a principal god. I empathise with that viewpoint. The raven seems to epitomise the spirit of the wilderness. On one occasion, sea kayaking in west Scotland, I had set up camp on a tiny island at the entrance to Loch Moidart. In the evening, I climbed to its highest point. As I looked out towards Mull and braced myself against the strong westerly wind, I was suddenly aware that, upwind and just below me, a raven hovered with wings spread as it too faced westward. As I was enjoying this moment, for I was used to seeing ravens at a distance above me, it suddenly disappeared like a bullet to the east. It seemed impossible that it could have seen me, as I was directly behind, above and downwind. Somehow, I knew that it had become aware of my presence. The following morning, I set off to kayak round the westerly headland of the island. The weather had deteriorated and the sea was rough. After some misgivings, I decided to carry on. As I rounded the low headland, to my astonishment there was a raven sitting no more than 20 metres away, watching me intently. I have no proof, but I know it was the same raven, and that it was getting its own back. "We can both play this game, of spying on each other."

Many years later, I was to have an even closer encounter with a raven. Having completed an interesting way up a Lakeland fell in winter, I sat on the top in the lee of some rocks. The weather was poor, with strong winds and rain. A raven landed no more than five metres away. They are quite common in the Lake District, but I had never expected to see one so close. I glanced at the silent, dark bird and could not resist calling "Quork, quork" in a loud voice. To my delight, not only did it reply, but our 'conversation' went on for two or three minutes. It was almost as if we were both saying, "so what if it is bad weather, let's enjoy meeting each other for this moment".[28]

Looking across this range of happenings that have had such a profound effect on me, there seem to be certain defining characteristics.

- There was always the sense that I was experiencing something I could never really understand let alone explain.

- They were unexpected and unpredictable. I would suggest therefore that trying to seek them would be counter-productive. I had hoped in my older and wiser years that my long, solo wilderness journeys would increase the likelihood of their happening, but I knew I could never make them happen. They were beyond control and more elusive than rainbows.

- They were timeless. The ego or conscious self was suspended; thinking was suspended. In terms of feelings – and words are inadequate here – individuality was replaced by a merging of performer and action, observer and observed, person and place.

- They were immeasurable, and yet I felt they were of elemental importance in any quest for happiness.

- The beauty of the experience was awe inspiring and unforgettable.

- They could happen anywhere. They might be expected especially to occur at places of worship, gardens and in the presence of artefact and architecture which intensely affect the emotions. Inevitably, because of my own enthusiasm for adventure and wilderness, I could see the latter as the major environment for such experiences, and especially when alone. It is possible that being aware that such experiences exist, spending time away from other people, and developing a natural skill and a sense of place may help to create an atmosphere where they occur.

The potential is there for anyone to experience these feelings – and probably at any stage of life – even though some people, through having developed or chanced upon an effective dimension of approach, may be more receptive than others.

Trying to categorise or even find appropriate words or phrases to describe these particular events unsurprisingly has presented problems. As I have said before, they seem to belong to a realm of truth or perennial wisdom that is beyond the logic of language. Poets and artists would use metaphor and symbols. In my search for an encompassing term I have used the word 'extraordinary', but this is too broad. 'Transcendent' may be more appropriate and has been used in similar contexts, as has 'spiritual' and 'mystical' and even 'magical'. F.C. Happold explores the notion of the mystical in his classic work on this subject, and in the accounts he brings forward for consideration there is a remarkably close correlation with the phenomena I have described.[29] In an earlier chapter I used the word spiritual to describe what is traditionally recognised as the most important aspect of being human. There is no doubt, for me at least, that all these experiences go deep into the spirit or essence of man, beyond or beneath the ego and conscious self. They are experiences of the spirit. 'Spirit', unlike 'spiritual', has wider connotations than just within the human world. The term is also commonly used outside of man as in 'spirit of place'.

Apt as these considered words may be for the author (and perhaps for some readers) they carry overtones of particular religions, philosophies or cults. I finally chose the term 'elemental' – a word that could be used to describe the basis or essence of being human and which has an accepted definition of 'pertaining to the forces of nature'.[30]

When trying to categorise the specific kinds of elemental experience, I am content to use the terminology of some of those who have worked with distinction in this field. The extraordinary moments I have previously described seem allied to what Jung termed 'moments of synchronicity'. These he defines as "meaningful coincidents in time".[31]

The second group of encounters, which lasted longer than moments but were still very transient, seemed to fit Abraham Maslow's description of 'peak experience'.[32] Whilst there have been many occasions over a lifetime in the outdoors when I have felt elation or exhilaration, the extraordinary dimension of flow, felt in a peak experience, has been absent.

The solo kayak journey in Alaska was patently neither a moment of synchronicity nor a peak experience, terms with which I had been long familiar. Eventually I found an answer, again in the work of Maslow. He pinpointed a state of being, different from his 'peak experience', which he termed 'high plateau'. This seemed to capture precisely what happened to me in Alaska. He wrote that such a state was characterised by "feelings of serenity" and could be achieved by "long hard work". The journey and the years of build-up to the solo Alaskan expedition did involve a considerable amount of effort. Then, almost a month of consistently feeling in a state of very deep contentment on the ocean was like being on a high plateau that I did not know even existed.

From my experience and knowledge, and from the accounts of others who adventure in the outdoors, it would appear that achieving this high plateau state of being is comparatively rare. Moments of synchronicity and peak experiences would seem to be more frequent. It may be that these feelings of complete harmony, especially with reference to the high plateau state, are more commonplace in other types of human activity. Of particular relevance here may be the experiences of people who have dedicated themselves to perfecting skills in the arts and crafts.[33] Similarly, those who make a living in a simple manner on the land or water and those who are deeply involved in spirituality and meditation share the aspect of a long commitment to task and place needed to make these special bonds.

Moments of synchronicity and peak experiences, according to measured time, are of short duration. When considering the high plateau state, however, I felt the concept of time itself was substantially different. The journey in Alaska and all my subsequent expeditions had absolutely nothing to do with any clock. Man-measured time was replaced by the rhythm of

Nature, of which dawn and dusk were but one facet. This is perhaps one aspect of major significance in the *perpetual* nature of this kind of experience. It would be a very unusual person who would not begin deeply to question what was happening to them in such a situation. Moments of synchronicity and peak experiences, in contrast, are so comparatively short lived that their significance may not be fully appreciated at the time or even subsequently. On the ocean in Alaska I seemed to merge with the natural rhythm and harmony of my surroundings. In a very real sense I was going back into Nature.

Happold uses the phase "a humble receptiveness" with reference to mystical experiences of this kind.[34] In Alaska, for me there was more than a sense of awe and wonder. There was a simple humility as I journeyed onwards, a sense that I was utterly privileged to be part of that wilderness. I was becoming a wanderer rather than an adventurer.

I still see myself as someone who is, and always has been, an enthusiast for action. My reflections on my actions, at least until middle age, tended to focus on matters of safety and quality of performance. What happened in Alaska was so powerful that I was compelled to try and understand it. By beginning to do so I came to realise that all these elemental experiences were part of the same radical message. *I was not separate from Nature.* It became irrelevant that for much of my life I might still feel the separateness of, 'I'm in here and everything else is out there'. This latter feeling is strongest now only when I am living in the modern world. It has all but disappeared when I'm out in the natural environment.

It is on this point that I wish to end the chapter. I had said previously that another person's experience is the plainest of shadows compared to one's own. Even if these examples of my own elemental experiences have captured the imagination of the reader, only I experienced and thus felt them. What I can do, however, and will do with confidence, is to ask the reader a question: "Have you ever had experiences in life, anywhere and at any time, where, if you thought about it, your feelings of separateness had somehow been suspended?"

I would be surprised if you were to answer in the negative.

CHAPTER 7

WILD FLOWERS AND TREKKING

A part from the central message of man's unity with wild nature, the Alaskan journey was to have considerable implications in terms of what I subsequently did in the outdoors with regard to recreation (re-creation). Directly, or indirectly, it was eventually to lead to glimmerings of understanding of other profound messages from nature, and to take me further on my inner journey. Looking back over those years I can see that I was no longer consciously making some important decisions. Instead they just seemed to happen, although I now believe my subconscious must have been in control. Allow me to explain what happened, before you are convinced that I have become incoherent.

From adolescence onwards, for over thirty years, I had been very strongly adventure-orientated. Being single-minded and determined to be successful, I had pursued a range of adventure activities one at a time. In turn, and over periods of years, I had committed myself to the adrenalin pursuits of rock climbing and mountaineering, white-water kayaking and catamaran sailing, surfing and, eventually, sea kayaking. Whilst the latter, especially when done solo, had led to increasing environmental awareness, it still had the central characteristic of the other activities. They were all exciting adventure sports, which in turn dominated my life. The decision to do each one was a *conscious* one. Then, one day, after the Alaskan trip, whilst following another adventure enthusiasm, that of solo rock scrambling, the following happened in Middlesteads Gill, above Thirlmere in the Lake District:

I approached the small steep ravine where the climb began. At its foot and directly in front of me was a tall plant with a magnificent deep blue flower. It impressed me, which was most unusual as I always ignored flowers. I then moved past, thinking how very vulnerable the flower would be if this particular scramble became popular, and concentrated on the climbing. As I scrambled over the top of the route, to my surprise there was another single flower of the same type. This time I studied the shape of the flower, again something I had never done before. It was so striking in appearance that I intuitively knew that I had never seen such a plant in the wild. I returned home in some excitement knowing that I wanted to find out what it was.

With the help of Annette, my wife, who is a keen botanist, and pictures in a flower guide, the mystery was quickly solved. It was a common Columbine. Odd, how words can debase a beautiful flower. Much better is the direct translation of its Latin name, *Aquilegia vulgaris*, the common Eagle-flower. I was later to find out that not only was this flower the state flower of Colorado, but it was a rare find growing in its wild form in the Lake District hills.

The finding of that flower was to lead directly to the development of a passion for wild flowers. Instead of my major outdoor interest being some form of physically demanding and exciting type of adventure, I suddenly wanted to be a successful amateur botanist.

At this point, you may wish to deduce that the writer was getting old, and in the natural process of things was moving away from physical adventure as a major commitment. I still had, however, a great enthusiasm for physical adventure, but that enthusiasm was for some years overtaken by searching for wild flowers.

Leaving aside for the moment the intriguing matter of why wild flowers suddenly dominated my life, let me describe what followed. I decided I would try to find as many different types of wild flowers as I could. After the inevitable difficulties of learning how accurately to identify them, I roamed northern England and Scotland for about two years to extend my master list. During that time I reluctantly let my friends and students know of my new enthusiasm. I use the word 'reluctantly' deliberately. My status and self-esteem, and my ego, were bound up with my expertise as an adventurer. It was difficult to respond to the common query of, "Where is your next expedition going to be?" with a reply concerned with a search for flowers in the UK!

Not being away on expedition that next summer meant that we, as a family, could plan an extended holiday. We decided on the Pyrenees, which fitted wonderfully with my new enthusiasm. The Spanish National Park of Ordessa as our first location could not have been a better choice. On a minor track high upon the south side of the main limestone canyon, we were to find the equivalent of the Garden of Eden. Not only was the immense variety of alpine flowers stunning, but somehow the arrangement of flowers seemed ordered in a way that was beyond the skills of any human gardener. Our walks on that and many other days were extremely slow, as we tried to identify every species. This was to be the beginning of many years of wilderness journeys, sharing in the delights of wild flowers with Annette.

After visiting other areas of the Pyrenees, including the granite of Sant Maurici and the limestone of Lescun, I returned home pleased and excited. I realised not only that I wanted wild flowers to be a major part of my life, but also that I had greatly enjoyed being back in the mountains. Climbing some of the peaks and crossing cols in both sunlight and storm had proved addictive. With early retirement in 1992, I had the freedom to expedition in the wilderness for long periods. As Annette was still working full time I often expeditioned alone, mainly in the Pyrenees, but with one particular journey across the French gorges and Alps with the twin objectives of covering a thousand miles and finding a thousand different wild flowers.

Throughout this period the aims were simple. I would travel as far as possible in a self-reliant manner, for example camping and not using huts, eating simply and not buying meals; and I would always plan to journey over ground with which I was unfamiliar. The Pyrenees were an ideal location for this style of travelling, as they were large, complex and, unlike much of the Alps, mainly wild. The conventional major routes along and across this mountain range were but a small fragment of possible journeys.*

The other aim was the obvious one. Each time I would try to find, identify and record as many different wild flowers as I could. Usually being alone, I was free to decide not only choice and length of route, but also how far I should travel each day. Most days began at dawn and varied between eight and twelve hours. During this period I trekked and climbed tens of thousands of both kilometres of distance and metres of ascent. Among the many different flowers found were several, including the Serapias Orchid and the Ground Pine which, according to the field guidebooks, were not supposed to grow in the Pyrenees. Inevitably the journeys were adventurous. They were also physically demanding.

To finish this descriptive section concerning these *outward* journeys, I want to focus on one day of particular importance to my inner journey. You will be aware, by now, that I have spent years doing a succession of

---

* For example, the following major routes: the crossing between Gavarnie and Ordessa, the 'Grande Randonnée 10' (GR10), the 'Gran Recorrido 11' (GR11) and the 'Haute Route Pyrenaica' (HRP).

different adventure activities. You may have already surmised that I moved on to a new activity each time because I was no longer progressing, or dare not progress, further. There is some truth in this. When I moved away from climbing after sixteen years, it was with a considerable feeling of depression. I could never remove the feeling that I was a failure or, to be more precise, a coward. Having climbed with some of the best climbers of the day, and knowing that compared with some of them I was at times climbing better than they were, I knew I lacked the will to try that bit harder. What made this feeling worse was that when on the odd occasion I had rejected my normal caution, and had really pushed myself, I had discovered that I was considerably more capable than I thought. That I did not continue to push myself was probably due to two reasons. The first and obvious one was that I was frightened of falling off. I had only fallen twice, once when leading an artificial climb and the other on snow and ice. The other reason was that the pressure to push further was, directly or indirectly, *competitive*. Something inside me has always strongly rejected competition as a major reason for climbing.

This feeling of failure in mountains was still with me in my travels in the Pyrenees, or at least until this particular day. I was doing an east-to-west solo traverse of the Spanish Pyrenees. By early June I had reached Bielsa and I suspected that I would be faced with the crux of the journey. Unseasonable amounts of snow from a bad winter had already given me some adventures, including one on the high Col Vallebierna over the shoulder of Pic Aneto. I travelled always as light as possible because of a knee that creaked even without a load on my back. Lack of an ice axe and crampons, with trackless terrain in the snow and ice conditions, had proved exciting. In a normal summer the conditions would have been much easier.

Walking up the road from Bielsa it was difficult not to be impressed by the long southern wall of the Pineta valley. Composed mainly of cliffs, the whole wall looked very steep and was never less than 1000 metres in height. It increased dramatically in height as it reared upwards to Monte Perdido, the highest peak in the Pyrenees. At the head of the valley, I pitched the tent and spent a fruitless and annoying afternoon trying to find the start of the route up the wall. I knew there was a path of some kind, even though the whole face seemed to say, "This area is not for walkers".

I left very early the next morning, both to give me time to find the way and in order to avoid the heat of the sun as I climbed. With relief, after two hours I eventually found the start of the route, but had to accept the energy-sapping heat. Footpath was the wrong description for the ascent. Keen eyes were essential in order to stay on the faintest of tracks, as it wove an intricate pattern up between the cliffs. Reaching the high Col Anisclo after many hours of hard work was a relief. From my eyrie, the view steeply back down to the valley floor, where I had previously pitched the tent, was very impressive. Relief at reaching the col, however, was short-lived. The red and white flashes marking the route had been few and far between, and any indicating the route westward were obliterated by a deep blanket of snow. Even without this problem, I knew this next section had an unhealthy reputation for being dangerous and exposed. To the west, beneath the col and me, lay the head of the Anisclo Canyon. I dismissed the idea of trying to descend into it. There appeared to be no path and it looked even more precipitous than the route I had ascended. I was later to find out that this was the route I should have taken, although it was not marked on my old map. After studying the complex mountain terrain above the head of the canyon, I reckoned I could see a line up the side of this main ridge of Monte Perdido which would take me west. The only other, and almost unthinkable, alternative seemed to be one of retreat.

Many hours later, and after much snow and ice work, using trekking poles for stability ("I must *not* fall"), and some scrambling, I finally reached the ridge itself at around 3000 metres. Heart in mouth, I looked down its western flank. Very relieved, I saw that I could descend its 200 metres of steep scree to a prominent limestone shelf. Once there, however, I found more problems. Beneath the shelf was another much larger shelf that I knew would contain the proper trail. Between the two, however, were vertical cliffs of at least 50 metres. I tried going north, along the upper shelf, for about a kilometre, but the cliffs only became larger. Despondently I retraced my steps and headed south. I was rapidly running out of options. A memory came floating in. Years ago in Torridon, in north-west Scotland, a group of students and I had trapped a pine marten in a series of vertical cracks on a small crag. Our aim had been to see this beautiful animal at close quarters, but I remember feeling guilty at causing the animal some stress. I was now beginning to feel like that pine martin!

After about 20 minutes going southwards along the upper shelf, I whooped for joy. Three small rocks on top of each other clearly indicated a cairn at the top of a rock cleft. A study of the cleft, however, left me despondent again. It was overhanging and apparently holdless. Rucksack off, I looked carefully down the buttress on its southern flank. It looked vaguely promising even though it was steep and exposed. The broad shelf lay invitingly about 50 metres below. Rucksack back on, I started climbing down. After about 20 metres or so, I became acutely conscious that I was at, or near, my climbing limits. Fortunately, the difficult moves, where both my balance and finger strength were severely tested, were confined to about 10 metres of the buttress. I was then able to escape leftwards on larger holds leading into the gully. Only a loose rock scramble remained to the foot of the cliffs.

My camp that night, by a tiny stream, on the platform that contained the path to the head of the Ordessa Canyon, seemed little short of wondrous. My food was scant and I was shattered, but I was happy. I sat outside the tent, almost oblivious to the piercing cold, and looked at the large moon over the Spanish plains to the south. I felt engulfed by the beauty of my surroundings.

I can see now that my senses were heightened both by having been in dangerous locations for many hours and because I had not seen another human being for two days. As important as the beauty of that evening, perhaps, was the feeling that I had at last exorcised the ghost of being a coward in the climbing situation. It was not so much the difficulty of the climb down, which was probably no more than Severe, but that I had not hesitated at the start of the descent. As to whether I got through having been more due to luck than anything else, I shall never know. Anyway, I suspect ultimately that this is irrelevant.

It was only after that particular experience that I came to love the mountains as I loved the sea. The barrier of fear no longer subconsciously ran riot when conditions became dangerous in the hills.

Chapter 8

FURTHER REFLECTIONS

If anyone had said to me, after my return from Alaska, that I would develop a passion for wild flowers, I would have dismissed the idea immediately as ridiculous. I had no interest in them, but when, very rarely, they had become a subject for discussion, I had been opposed to time spent on such frivolity, particularly in the mountains. On the expedition to Trivor in the Karakoram, for example, most of us who had gone to climb were unhappy that we had a member of the team whose only task was botanical exploration. This was the famous botanist Oleg Polunin. I now deeply regret my lack of botanical interest and the wasted opportunity, both of his company and of an area unexplored botanically.

At that time, it seemed to me sensible that everyone should be committed to climbing the peak. I held and displayed a similar attitude years later, when attending the first Mountaineering Instructor's Advanced Certificate assessment course at Plas y Brenin, the National Mountaineering Centre. Whilst out 'on expedition', I was asked by Johnny Lees, the assessor, to identify a small yellow flower on the hillside. My reply was combative, and to the effect that I did not know, did not care, and that mountains were for climbing. That my wife loved flowers merely convinced me it was a feminine pastime.

Lest you are in any doubt, let me stress that searching for wild flowers *suddenly* became my *major* enthusiasm for at least two years, and in that time any physical adventure activity was comparatively unimportant. This love of flowers, especially in the wild, has been an unexpected highlight of my later years, and complementary to the quest for physical adventure.

The question of the origin of this sudden and unexpected passion I find fascinating. I can only conclude that, somehow, something in my unconscious marked 'flowers' surfaced. I used a similar expression when trying to explain what happened in Alaska (i.e. "… that part of me that was the ocean was somehow switched on"). I then went on to describe the 'oceanic feeling' of a high plateau experience. My love of flowers, however, has never been a high plateau experience. Neither have there been any peak

75

experiences. Indeed the only elemental experience concerning flowers has been a recent single moment of synchronicity.

Early one morning I had gone into the garden to hang a towel on the line. As I did so, I was instantly aware of a powerful presence hitting me in the back– not physically, but psychologically. If that does not make sense, then in a way it doesn't matter, because I now intuitively know that at least some of the most profound experiences are beyond rational description. I turned round, but I think I already knew the cause. The impulse had come from a group of garden pansies that looked beautiful in the early morning sunshine. Somehow, I knew they were rebuking me for not acknowledging their presence as I had walked past them. I silently expressed my apologies as I admired them. I had been half-asleep and too wrapped up in my own thoughts.

What I find amusing, and perhaps typical of Nature as manifest in this experience, is that I had literally spent years looking for wild flowers in the wilderness with complete enthusiasm and always hoping for some special experience. Yet, never on any of those expeditions and with all those lovely flowers had there been such a moment of synchronicity.

Returning to the matter of the *origin* of this new activity, I wonder whether my unconscious deliberately impelled me into it or, to put it a different way, as Nature and I are one, there was a message of the following kind coming from deep within:

"You have spent too much of your life on self-centred physical adventure. You still lack awareness and respect for the physical environment around you, except where it concerns your safety and desire for success. You have essentially been using the wilderness as an extension of the sports hall. It may be that you do not do much damage to it, but you have been largely blind to its elemental messages as to who you are. I am therefore going to give you a shock. You are going to commit yourself to something that has no manly status, is not necessarily physically demanding and is not adrenalin-dependent. I hope you learn deeply from this new stage."

Writing this now, at least fifteen years since the onset of this new phase of my inner journey, I feel I have begun to learn. But it is only a beginning. In the first instance there is the message, 'never presume you know yourself completely, no matter how much the extent of your experience'. This would seem to emphasise an approach to life of humility rather than of arrogance. In the second instance, there is something here of profound importance concerning beauty. There can be few better illustrations of the concept 'small is beautiful', for example, than the world of alpine flowers. I now never fail to be excited by this magical world. High in the mountains, and not least in rocky and dangerous places, exquisite flowers grow. I still find it both amazing and wonderful that such places, so subject to storm and extremes of temperature, can harbour such perfection in Nature. How much I now regret all those earlier years in the hills and other wild places when I was so immersed in my own adventures that I was blind to so much beauty.

It is worth looking further at the notion of blindness. Initially you are blind in the sense of being completely unaware, if there is not the motivation or enthusiasm to *want* to see. Or if, as in my case, preoccupation with the values of one area of activity actually precluded attention being given to those of another. Once that hurdle has been overcome you can be faced with another, more practical problem. You look, but do you see? I suspect that, in every sense, we miss far more than we realise. We perhaps need only to consider the extreme abilities of some non-human life forms to see or to be aware in other senses (for example, an insect's perception of polarised light), or to consider the heightened ability of a blind person to hear or feel, to emphasise the point. I know from my own experience of looking for flowers that I do not see all that is before my eyes, even now. The way the Fly Orchid can disappear into the background when you know it is there is an example.

Seeing, of course, is just one of the basic senses. Intuitively, I feel that all these senses are of importance far beyond their practical and immediate value. The more they can be developed, and the wilderness environment is the natural place in which to do this, the more we can relate to that to which we belong.

I wonder also if there are basic senses beyond the conventional five of seeing, hearing, smelling, tasting and touching. And further, that if there are, do we really appreciate how important they might be? Two possible additions come to mind. The first is an kinaesthetic sense, which might best be described as the feeling of 'bodily movement having a natural and highly satisfying rhythm'. The second is a sense of awe and wonder, a sense of the existence of something *beyond* ourselves. Without this sense I feel certain that a human being cannot hope to develop inwardly. Neither can she or he hope, therefore, to find enduring contentment. Such a sense is perhaps more profound than the other basic senses. It can lead directly into feelings of beauty and into the core, or heart, of being human. In that process it can have a direct effect on how the world is perceived and a major effect on what is valued.

If the sense of wonder, in examples such as seeing and appreciating the perfection and beauty of flowers, is of profound importance, then there needs to be a corresponding awareness of the relative *unimportance* of the ego. By this I do not mean dismissal of the ego, even if that were possible. The ego, or aspect of conscious self, is an inevitable and basic part of being human. The problem seems to be when the ego assumes domination. Self-centredness leads to blindness concerning key messages from Nature. When trying to find wild flowers, for example, I can now see that my ego would try to exert its importance. I would take immature pleasure in being the first to find a particular flower when, as a naïve beginner, I was in the company of experts. A particular example comes to mind. I was in the Eastern Pyrenees with professional botanists who were sharing their wild flower finds, using Latin names. I wandered off, feeling very inadequate, and happened to find a particular orchid. The local professor had searched for this flower for about twenty years. He was not amused! Both our responses were derived from feelings of competition and acquisition rather than from attention to the flower itself.

The same was true when I wrote to the author of a reputable flower guide to point out that particular alpine flowers were not absent from the Pyrenees. Keeping detailed records of flower recordings from each journey, and setting myself challenges like 'finding a 1000 different wild flowers on an Alpine trip', were also examples of the ego at work. Fortunately, I grad-ually became aware that all these egocentric aims were unimportant. The initial enjoyment and satisfaction, if not excitement, came from finding a new flower. Nature is delightful in her many surprises, and you cannot begin to know the pleasure of discovery until you experience it. This is followed by appreciating the beauty of the flower, at first in its entirety and then in the details of its parts during the challenge of identification. Once this is accurately achieved, the door is open to further knowledge. The aesthetic appreciation of the beauty of the flower is naturally followed by the desire to get to know it, and the skill of identification. I can now fully understand why flowers are such an enduring and rewarding aspect of human living.

In one way the conscious decision to take up walking and trekking was almost as surprising as being impelled into the world of flowers. Certainly my view for a long time was that it was essentially an activity that was, in that keyword of adolescence, *boring*. Walking used to be reluctantly accepted by me as the unavoidable means to reach the climb. It was a pursuit that was for those who had a minimal spark of adventure or, worse, for those who did not dare to adventure. Writing such statements now makes me feel distinctly uncomfortable. They are not only a reflection of considerable arrogance. They also reflect a blinkered approach to both the values of, and the serious adventures that can be found within, this encompassing activity. It was to take years of intensive journeying before I began to appreciate something of its elemental values.

Before I look at some of the deeper values, however, it would be sensible to look briefly at the adventure potential of trekking in comparison to more *sensational* forms of adventure such as rock climbing and white-water canoeing. All forms of adventure out of doors have the same basic element – like life itself – of being journeys with a degree of uncertainty. In its more extreme forms, walking can be a dangerous pastime. Anyone caught in a storm on British hills, especially in winter, will recognise this fact. On bigger mountains the objective dangers, those over which one has no control, can easily make walking an adventure of considerable risk. Such risks are accentuated if one journeys alone.

In all these examples, however, walking or trekking becomes directly similar to other types of adventure. A degree of danger and exposure releases adrenalin, a chemical agent, into the body. As is well known, the heightened state of awareness and physical capability as a result of this hormone gives scope for improved performance. I would wish, however, to take this matter further. Consider the situation where the trekker is alone, is extremely tired from prolonged effort, but is still far away from a haven of any kind. There may be no excitement involved, the scenery may be dull, or in any event you are past caring about it, and there is nothing of the interesting movements of more dynamic forms of adventure or a sudden problem to occupy your mind. You just have to 'keep on keeping on'. In such situations, I suspect that overcoming the challenge can be harder than the climb or passage through white water. There is no adrenalin to assist your performance. It is a matter of sheer physical effort along with control of those negative feelings that threaten to overpower you with persistent messages of stopping.

Certainly, I now value walking as a major form of recreation because of its strong physical demands and the occasional exciting adventures on the way. I might have an idea when the latter may occur as I plan a journey, but nature is never predictable. Such events are often unexpected, and especially so in trackless terrain.

I had moved away from seeking immediate adrenalin adventure situations. Even though I often enjoyed those experiences when they arrived on a journey, I was no longer adrenalin dependent. This would seem to be important in terms of beginning to understand how one relates to one's surroundings. Adrenalin, even though natural, is a drug, and because of that fact it is very easy to be consumed by it. There is something of a paradox here. Adrenalin is an essential aid for survival and for peak performance. It can also lead to great rewards in terms of elation and other feelings of well-being.* On the other hand, because it has so powerful an effect on bodily functions, it can massively fuel the ego. If adrenalin is involved in order to achieve success, rather than survival, then it is easy to become consumed by what might be termed the 'look at me and what I have done' factor. This is, of course, an egotistical or self-centred road.

I need at this point to elaborate on what I mean by self-centred. It is the normal condition of the modern human being, as it presupposes we are all separate from everything around us. It was how I felt before the 'high plateau' experience of Alaska. The combination of searching for wild flowers and long wilderness solo-backpacking was to reinforce the feeling of oneness, rather than of separateness from my natural surroundings.

As I journeyed over those thousands of miles and crossed over almost endless series of mountain cols, a question would often surface:

"Why am I doing this activity when I do not instinctively like walking?"

Somehow the beauty of both the landscape and flora and fauna, combined with the physical and sometimes psychological challenge of the journey itself, seemed insufficient as an answer. Yet even as I asked myself this question, deep down I knew there was an inner contentment. This was to such a degree that even the joy of being home was, after a few days or so, replaced by the desire to plan the next journey. Very gradually I realised that my whole approach to the outdoors was changing. I wanted simply to walk through and explore the wilderness as a way of life.

---

* The post-adrenalin phase allows access to a different way of experiencing the physical world. Decomposed adrenalin is a chemical almost identical to the drug LSD.

CHAPTER 9

A PILGRIM IN THE WILD

To be an adventurer is to be one who seeks out, and then tries to overcome, a challenge. Those who are attracted to such adventures in the wilderness are numbered in their millions, and I had been one of them. Now, however, I no longer regard such challenges as the principal reason for adventurous journeys. Admittedly I still set myself specific aims for each journey I undertake, but these are not now of prime importance. The adventures encountered, whilst often being the highlight and intensely satisfying, are similarly unimportant. What is now more important is living in, and moving through, the wilderness with eyes wide open and mind alert. Over many expeditions, some lasting up to three months, it has become natural to accept the diversity of terrain and weather, and the demands involved. I realised that what was satisfying was simply journeying through wild places, as self-reliantly as possible. Effort, and sometimes struggle, were inevitable. Not only was that accepted, but I eventually realised that, as I approached a col or a summit, I was almost sorry that the struggle was over.[35]

My contentment on those expeditions was in part because I did not feel lonely. The reason was simple. I was surrounded by all my friends. This may sound odd, for I was usually alone. But I'm referring here to my friends in the natural environment. An essential insight had finally surfaced into my consciousness: *"Everything in nature is alive in its own way."* Somehow I now accepted implicitly that *all* aspects of nature, whether on a macro or micro scale, had their own being. This included, for example, the rocks and the clouds, the rivers and the stars, as well as the flora and fauna. You may have difficulty in accepting these statements. It would seem ridiculous to ascribe 'aliveness' to a rock, for example. I do not pretend to understand how a rock can be 'alive in its own way' and I regret that I can give no scientific explanation. Yet I remain completely convinced of the truth of this matter. Perhaps the word 'alive' in this context may be more easily accepted if paraphrased as 'having a way of being'.

For those who doubt this perception, it is worth considering that, in the first instance, there is far more about life that we do *not* know, than we do know. "There are more things in heaven and earth, Horatio, than are dreamt of in your philosophy."[36] It is yet another wisdom, that the more we know, the more we find there is to know. An open-hearted, open-minded approach to life is essential if we are to progress on an inner journey.

On a winter trek in the Pennines, I arrived at a small, quiet village. To my delight, for it was early on a Sunday morning, I was invited in by a local for a cup of tea. He was a retired stonemason and during the conversation I could not resist asking him the following question, "In your lifetime of working with many types of rock, have you ever considered rock to be alive?" He looked at me with some amusement and I thought I had been stupid. His reply was wisdom itself, "Yes, of course rock is alive."

I left refreshed, not only by his tea but by his answer. I was later to reflect that there were probably many human beings who work with the basic materials of nature, who would have a similar viewpoint. My thinking hence moved me onwards. The original statement of wisdom was too restricted. It needed expansion: *"Everything in nature is alive in its own way, and seeks well-being."* Even for a rock there is a 'good way to be'.

I see no natural reason, for example, why all forms of life that can, should not play as well as work to survive. Descending beneath a cliff in a wild part of the Pyrenees, my youngest daughter and I were treated to a magnificent display by a bird called a wall-creeper. For several minutes it went up, down and round the vertical cliff face above us. We watched fascinated. I remember wondering at the time if it was deliberately giving us a display rather than hunting for food. I also wondered, much later, if birds have egos!

I have often seen both puffins and gulls playing in the wind where a gale hits the face of a sea cliff. They were certainly not seeking food. Ravens, too, are well known for their playful and carefree antics. I have also seen seals playing on reefs in big seas. All these living creatures seemed to be expressing that freedom and joy in their environment that the human being craves.

Whilst the majority might accept that animals in general, have such aims, I feel it is likely to be true of all life forms. I find no difficulty with accepting that plants seek their own states of well-being. Why should humans arrogantly dismiss this possibility and confine the assessment of plants to cold rational and scientific explanations as to their state of existence? Books such as *The Secret Life of Plants*[37] strongly suggest otherwise. In a science-based society where proof is regarded as essential, these ideas are dismissed as those of cranks. The possibility that plants have feelings is ridiculed because it directly challenges the conventional viewpoint. Yet it is worth noting that many of the world's great inventions have come directly from unconventional thinking. Any green-fingered gardener, for example, knows consciously or subconsciously that the well-being of the plant is dependent as much on a good relationship as upon the accepted necessities for optimum growth.[38]

When it comes to the well-being of apparently inert aspects of nature, I am obviously on contentious ground. Yet I must persevere because I feel it intuitively to be true. There is no way I can logically, or rationally, explain it. In a sense this gives me little cause for concern for I suspect that it is another wisdom from Nature that there will always be the inexplicable. Walt Whitman recognised this aspect in his poetry, "I do not know it … it is without name … it is a word unsaid, It is not in any dictionary or utterance or symbol."[39] If we lose the sense of the inexplicable and mystery of nature, then we would lose our sense of awe and wonder about it. It could be that this sense is essential in our journey in life if we are even to *begin* to understand.

Consider the following. It is understandable that the man-made world needs basic resources for efficient living in conurbations and cities, for recreation and for efficient means of travel. Convenience, speed of travel and short-termism are major factors in the decision-making process. Behind these factors lurk the major aspects of finance and profit opportunities. Nearly all these decisions are, in practice, human-centred. There may be occasional acknowledgement of the importance of a particular environment to the point where a traffic scheme may be re-routed or even suppressed. There may also be strong defence of an area by eco-warriors. In general, however, the man-made juggernaut moves onwards. It is highly convenient for the moneymakers, and maybe even the planners, to use the natural world essentially as a resource for human advantage. There is very little official thought given to the well-being of everything in nature. Even in the case of national parks, preservation of the landscape is seen to be important as a direct benefit to people, rather than for its own sake.* The

---

* A recent ban on access to the mountains where I live prompted a friend to comment on how she found a strange new pleasure in looking at them, appreciating an added beauty in their enforced isolation.

result is a planet littered with examples of the greed and ignorance of the human race. I feel very strongly that the human being should disturb Nature only in as minimal a way as possible. The high plateau experience I underwent in Alaska convinced me of my unity with nature. To destroy anything in Nature, unless for survival and basic human living, is, in reality, to harm ourselves.

Towards the end of my first Alaskan expedition, before we finished at Sitka, both Barry and I went fishing He had gone up the small river on the island and I had gone offshore. I fished from the kayak in some reefs and caught a substantial fish, a red snapper. Weather deteriorated suddenly and prudence dictated a quick return to land. With difficulty I got the fish aboard and placed it under the strong deck elastics in front of me. As I paddled towards the shore, the fish flapped desperately in a frenzy to escape. I could not avoid watching its death throes. By the time I landed, I swore I would never fish again unless my survival depended upon it. The fish had unnecessarily died, as I had food, and I had become distraught. We had both suffered from the experience.

Nature and the human being are indivisible. Yet because of the profit motive and lack of awareness, the unnecessary destruction of Nature continues apace. On a global scale there are already graphic indications of a payback in terms of natural disasters and major problems for the modern human race.

If all aspects of Nature are alive in their own way and seek well-being, then it would seem eminently possible that they are also on their own self-reliant adventurous journeys. Emerson's idea of Nature allowing nothing to survive unless it is self-reliant seems a truism, even if there is also much counterbalancing evidence of various life forms working together. The idea of other life forms adventuring may seem odd, but this is perhaps due to the irrational and arrogant view that 'adventure' is essentially a human activity. In the human world much adulation is given to those who successfully explore frontiers and live their lives along the sharp edge. It is important for humans to realise that most of modern man's achievements have been accomplished in conjunction with a reliance on all the latest technological resources. There are many other life forms that make adventurous journeys on a quite remarkable scale, without such resources and probably without any form of adulation from their own kind. Study of migratory birds, for example, has shown that they prepare very carefully for expeditions. The dangers facing them can be severe. It is well known that the swallow population often has been decimated in the annual journeys between Africa and Western Europe. It is also well known that certain species of terns annually make remarkable journeys between northern Europe and the southern latitudes.

There are innumerable examples from other migratory life forms. A species of eel takes years to go from the Sargasso Sea to the rivers of Europe. Further north, the magnificent salmon travels between Greenland and its spawning grounds in the rivers of Europe. Further west, the monarch butterfly journeys south across the bulk of the American states. As it goes south, so a species of moth goes east across the Atlantic to Europe. In the ocean depths scientists are beginning to discover that certain species of whales cover enormous distances. As our knowledge increases, the list becomes almost endless.

When it comes to thinking of plants and trees having adventurous journeys the imagination may be stretched. A dismissive view of them would tend to regard them as comparatively static. Yet seeds travel in many ingenious ways, and if one can imagine being such a life form then I do not think it is that difficult to accept that they have an adventure before them. There is a description by John Muir of an ancient but very small, gnarled tree, the Dwarf Pine, high on a ridge in the Rockies.[40] Imagine being in such a place for hundreds of years facing the challenge of storms and winter conditions. I marvel as well at the not dissimilar challenges faced by tiny alpine flowers. If adventure can be described as 'a journey with a degree of uncertainty' and one that is in a natural environment involving hardship and danger, then it is worth knowing that many life-forms, other than humans, are on similar journeys.

You may query whether this knowledge is of relevance to the inner journey of a human being. The answer must surely be affirmative. Knowing about such journeys should increase our awareness of and respect for the natural environment. It can also increase our sense of awe and wonder. Imagine being a water droplet that has come from the ocean, travelling cloud-high over the globe and then descending into a mountain stream to join the tumultuous journey back to the sea!

My increasing awareness of such adventures, coupled to the immense and diverse beauty that surrounded my own journeys, must have significantly contributed to realising another wisdom: *"I am no more and no less important than anything else in Nature"*.

I'm not at all sure I understood the extreme significance of this statement when I first intuitively accepted it as an eternal truth. Over the years, however, my difficulty with the concept has diminished. Indeed, I feel it is typical human arrogance to think otherwise. The human race may be extremely clever and very powerful as a species, but I would question whether contentment and happiness are the common condition. "The mass of men lead lives of quiet desperation".[41] I would also question why the human race has enacted so much unnecessary devastation of its natural surroundings. This behaviour makes me severely question *any* concept of human superiority over the rest of Nature.

There is also another way of looking at this problem. It seems sensible that whatever life for man is about, it should include the maximum development of the individual, in all senses of being human, within an acceptable social and environmental frame. In other words, the human should be striving for, or progressing towards, the ideal of perfection. Everything in nature too is probably striving for perfection. If asked to give an example of this perfection, or near perfection, then I would think of a tiny flower, a raindrop or a blade of grass. There have been many heroes and heroines, but I would hazard a guess that the majority of them would be the first to admit that they were a long way from approaching perfection.

If one looks at this wisdom concerning equality in a purely human context, then it means that no human being is more important than any other human being. I smile when I write this, and imagine that it would not receive universal assent. I smile less when I look in the mirror. There was a long stage in my working life when I thought I was irreplaceable. Many of us in the human world have a formidable journey to make.

Accepting the importance of equality in nature was to affect my attitude to life radically. I have, I hope, moved considerably away from the very self-centred or egocentric attitudes of my youth. Then, after many years of a combination of self-centredness and human-centredness, where I had placed great emphasis on teaching and helping others to adventure, I became essentially eco-centred. I do not particularly like the term, but if I am anything now, it is an 'ecosopher', which means literally 'seeker of earth wisdom'. My dislike of it is because, like 'philosopher', it has connotations of considering oneself important when all that matters in this context is giving as honestly as one can one's own testament of experience. I now have a deep concern for the whole of Nature as well as its individual aspects.

To end this chapter, I want to turn to what may be the most profound of all wisdom derived from Nature. I have previously described the spiritual centre of the human being as 'the most important aspect of being human'. I also suggested that this was a wisdom that could be traced back in human history, and that various words had been used to describe it, such as 'heart', 'soul' and 'conscience'. I now believe that there is something deeper within the centre – "a sense sublime of something far more deeply interfused".(42) I would describe this as *transcendent spirit* or *essence*. I came across these terms when preparing for the lecture tour in New Zealand in 1998. What this seems to mean is, firstly, that the spiritual centre has no boundaries. It goes on for ever and is therefore infinite. Secondly, this 'essence' is completely beyond any feelings of, or concepts about, separation. It is transcendent, beyond existence in the sense of physical life, and leads into and provides a world of unity, harmony, serenity and radiance.

It may be obvious why I was so excited about this discovery. Almost certainly, I had come across these terms in previous reading many years earlier, but their significance had escaped me. With long experience in the wilderness, and especially the elemental experiences and reflections upon them, I sensed intuitively that this was an eternal truth. The concept seemed to follow naturally from the other wisdoms I have mentioned – not only that, it also gave me joy. Those closest of friends, who had died in my early years, in an *essential* sense were, and always would be, around. I do not wish to be fanciful in this most profound of areas, but I can recall occasions when, in a time of stress in the outdoors, I have felt their presence.

On an equally happy note I could look at the work of any human being through resources such as libraries and art galleries, with the knowledge that their creators exist in the most meaningful of senses. Perhaps, in an ultimate sense, there is simply no beginning and no end. This ultimate truth of essence, then, links everything in Nature into an infinite unity. I find it very difficult to put into words anything about this most profound of subjects. Indeed even *thoughts* of this inmost depth within myself make me feel inadequate. My reverence for this concept, however, is total. I take heart from the fact that this wisdom has existed throughout human history, and that there are and have been human beings who could begin to express its profundity:

"All that man has eternally here in multiplicity, is intrinsically *one*. Here all blades of grass, wood, stone, all things are *one*. This is the deepest depth."[43]

Meister Eckhart (1260–1328)

"All creatures are the same life, the same presence, the same power, the same one and nothing else."[44]

Henry Suso (1295–1366)

"… if you inhibit thought (and persevere), you come at length to a region of consciousness below and behind thought … and a realisation of an altogether vaster Self than that to which we are accustomed. And since the ordinary consciousness with which we are concerned in ordinary life is before all things founded on the little local self … it follows that to pass out of that is to die to the ordinary self and the ordinary world.

It is to die in the ordinary sense, but in another sense it is to wake up to find that the 'I', one's real, most intimate self, pervades the universe and all other beings … that the mountains, and the sea, and the stars, are part of one's body … and that one's soul is in touch with all creatures."[45]

Edward Carpenter (1844–1929)

Many of our ancestors, living basic and harsh lives, and surrounded by both danger and beauty, knew this wisdom. This may also apply to many traditional peoples striving to preserve their cultures in the present world. In both cases, the lifestyles are often condemned as uncivilised. My impression is that they were, or are, much happier in their brief, simple lives than most modern human beings with all their affluence and convenience living. And for all the sophisticated refutations that suggestion may attract, it is a view to which, instinctively, I hold.

CHAPTER 10

SEEKING UNITY WITH NATURE

In an earlier chapter I put forward the idea that the central, most important, message from the University of the Wilderness was that we all have the potential to be aware of the unity we have with our natural surroundings. To those who would reply "Why bother?", I would say, first, that to feel that unity, to have that 'oceanic feeling', is to be transported to a level of contentment considerably beyond the deeply satisfying feelings basic to adventure in the outdoors. Whilst there are other powerful reasons to try to find this unity, my concern here is to offer ideas which may assist the search. I use the word 'ideas' deliberately because I know that my awareness of this state came from elemental experiences. In other words I could not plan for this to happen. These experiences were, for me at least, a rare occurrence. Not only that, it took years before I realised their essential message.

There may well be some very fortunate individuals who have not lost, or who have rediscovered, the gift of the very young to go into the natural environment and spontaneously feel at one with their surroundings. Such people, however, are likely to be very much in the minority. For most people, the common condition is that of separateness, if not alienation, from everything around them. 'I am in here and everything else is out there' is the common feeling, especially in our modern, developed world.

As a first step away from that feeling or condition of alienation, it is worth keeping in mind the fact that we are all part of Nature. Even if one lives in the middle of the city, and work is entirely concerned with the technological world, this fact is inescapable. Each of us, for the present at least, has arrived on the planet through a *natural* process. We are all natural creations and, whether we like it or not, we are inseparable from Nature. Whilst this may be fact, however, I do not suppose that many even give it a thought. In situations of stress and danger especially they are likely to feel the opposite.

As a second step to seeking this unity, it is worth trying to see what are the defining characteristics of Nature. As each of us is essentially 'natural', these characteristics may be of considerable help in our search. I feel this to be of particular importance in a world where there is a vast literature on the subject of 'how to find happiness'. Whilst it is useful to have a great deal of choice on what to read and learn around this topic, the sheer volume of material is daunting. It is often difficult to sift out the worthwhile, and sometimes difficult to assess the integrity of the writer in an area where 'spiritual materialism' is a constant threat.* In addition to these problems, some of the most profound writing can be difficult to comprehend.

The characteristics of Nature I am going to put forward to the reader here have come from reflecting over a lifetime in the outdoors, and especially from the concept and experience of the adventurous journey.

From within the vast complexity of Nature, I discern three key *pillars of wisdom*. They are akin to signposts that point the way as we journey through life. To ignore, underestimate or misunderstand any of them may well result in a diminution of our hopes of finding any enduring feelings of contentment.

First Pillar: Uncertainty

Everything in Nature is dynamic. Nothing stands still. Technological progress is unlikely ever to remove uncertainty. Power and riches cannot alter the fact that life, for everyone, is an uncertain journey. From Ecclesiastes and the pre-Confucian *I Ching* ('The Book of Changes' from the 12th century BC) right down to Thomas Wolfe's "The essence of life is flow not fix"[46] – literature has recognised this truth.

At first sight this characteristic of Nature may not seem helpful in a search for unity. The reverse, however, is true. If uncertainty is a key facet of Nature, the individual always has a choice. He or she can face life, both in the immediate and long-term senses, either in a *positive* or a *negative* manner. Most of us perhaps sway between the two extremes, depending on a range of factors, not least those of motivation or enthusiasm for any situation we are in or decision we have to take. My concern here, however, is in the broad sense of an approach to life. There is a marked tendency for modern man to seek increasing convenience and security, where the ideal human situation is seen as one where there is a minimum of effort and no risk. Such an

---

* This is the term used by Chögyam Trungpa to describe a distorted, ego-centred version of spirituality. See *Cutting Through Spiritual Materialism* by Chögyam Trungpa, Shambala Dragon Editions, Boston & London 1987

approach to life is not only negative and unnatural, but likely to lead to anxiety. The positive approach to uncertainty has to be the appropriate and productive way forward, an approach that accepts a state of being which Keats termed, 'Negative Capability': "Negative Capability, that is when man is capable of being in uncertainties, mysteries, doubts, without any irritable reaching after fact and reason …".[47]

In making these statements I could equally have said that *adventure* is the central and crucial factor in the approach to life. If anything defines adventure, then it is an acceptance that life is a journey with a degree of uncertainty.

A lifetime of working in adventure activities across the age ranges has convinced me that there is an *instinct* for adventure. If this is true, then that instinct has to find outlets. Those in positions of authority in both government and education systems need to accept, and work towards, a situation where *all* young people have the opportunity to be involved in adventure to the level of facing natural dangers, in a natural environment, and in a self-reliant manner. I know from experience that suitably trained teachers with a careful and progressive approach based on the capabilities of each *individual* young person could ensure an efficient safety framework.

Alfred North Whitehead rightly placed adventure as part of the basis of any civilised society, along with peace, art, beauty and truth. Indeed, he went further and wrote, "Without adventure civilisation is in full decay".[48] Approaching life, then, in an adventurous rather than negative manner is the *natural* way forward.

Second Pillar: Energy

The concept of energy underlies all we know about the Universe. Energy, effort and skills are basic to being alive. Many life forms expend tremendous energy and display magnificent skills as they journey with a natural grace through life.* In theory, the message from Nature is both simple and elemental. Spare nothing in your efforts to develop progressively all your being. As you journey, accept that there will always be trials and tribulations along the way, and that further horizons will always beckon.

The implication is obvious. The potential to perform at your individual highest levels exists within you, but their attainment demands energy, effort

---

* The essence of the book *Jonathan Livingstone Seagull.*

and skill. More than that, the modern person needs to recognise that other life forms achieve their highest levels of performance because they continuously and entirely live, work and play in a natural environment. *Their whole life is natural.* Modern man has the problem of having to devote considerable time and energy to living and working in a technological world, with its unnatural rhythms. To reach the highest levels of performance demands repeated and progressive practice, to the stage where the skills become second nature. The actions have to become as easy as walking down the road. Efficiency and rhythm in arduous and difficult situations are the result of living the activity and years of striving.

For human beings, excellence is reached at, or near, the edge of one's capabilities. Such commitment brings its own rewards. Satisfaction can lead to deeper feelings of elation when performing with grace and rhythm in testing situations. In all the inevitable frustrations, however, of trying to improve competence in an activity, and especially in those flat periods when skills seem to stagnate, it is worth remembering that vitality and style still matter.

Third Pillar: Balance

Everything in Nature is striving to achieve balance, from the stars in the heavens to the tiniest forms of life. Once even faintly sensed, this fact seems breathtaking. A study of the movement of tides and tidal streams, for example, whether for the British Isles or globally, reveals an amazing diversity which blends together. Studies of the winds of the world reveal the same. In some wonderful way the whole of the natural world is a self-regulating system in a dynamic equilibrium. In this concept of Gaia, which I intuitively recognise as truth, each organism has to find a niche if it is to survive.[49] The system works through a complex series of interrelationships at every level. Competition for survival is inevitable, but it is kept in balance as part of the whole. Co-operation is an equally fundamental concept in this respect. It is man's technological tampering with natural systems on an extreme scale that threatens this global equilibrium.

In more recent years, as I have journeyed in wild places there has been a constant deep feeling of contentment. I now realise this feeling is due to more than the satisfaction from being on an adventure. It essentially stems from returning to, and being absorbed by, the magnificent rhythm of Nature. When I look at my approach to the outdoors in my younger days, I can see little of this connection with Nature. I had no idea of the balance of the natural world and neither did I feel consciously that I was part of it. I also, and very significantly, misunderstood competition.

In the case of man, not only can competition – at any level – encourage separateness and divisiveness but it can also work against any feelings of unity with Nature. The common tendency after overcoming a difficult challenge is, subconsciously at least, to say "Look at *me*. Look what *I* have achieved" and "Aren't *I* great!", or "Look at *us*. Look what *we* have achieved" and "Aren't *we* great!" What is happening here is that a basic aspect of being human, the ego, is taking over. There are always moments to delight in being separate, and to bask in feelings of accomplishment and superiority. It is a rare person who, in these moments, reflects that they are at one with Nature. But to allow the ego persistently to dominate is to destroy any possibility of a unity with Nature. Yet the temptations to do just that are very considerable. Imagine you are progressing to world-class level in a major sport or adventure activity. At every stage in your progress there is increasing publicity and adulation. You are becoming a star and increasingly famous. At these levels an inflated ego is commonplace, but the temptations are there for most of us. The greater man's achievement, the more the need there is for humility rather than the egoism of arrogance.

Egoism destroys the balance within a person. It also demonstrates a marked lack of awareness of man's place in the great scheme of natural existence. If we can follow these three pillars of wisdom from the wilderness and accept life as an adventure, work and play with unremitting effort and skill, accept the inner importance of balance within oneself and in Nature, then a magical feeling of unity with Nature becomes a distinct possibility.

If I look beyond adventure into this world of unity, I would see mirrored the simple word, *beauty*. Keats well understood its profound importance:

"'Beauty is truth, truth beauty,'– that is all
    Ye know on earth, and all ye need to know".[50]

What I feel here – and I only have glimmerings of understanding – is that beauty and unity are synonymous. In other words, to experience beauty is, upon reflection, to experience feelings of connection. In some mysterious way, experiencing this kind of beauty creates a bond or relationship between the spiritual centre of man and Nature. During that experience, feelings of separateness are suspended. Nansen wrote, "Anything more wonderfully beautiful than the Polar night does not exist. It is a light poem of all the finest and most delicate tones of the soul."[51]

If this idea is true, then beauty, like unity, is the central message from Nature. It is particularly pertinent to the adventurer. If one looks carefully at the demands of adventure, one particular and crucial aspect of being human is often not valued. The challenge may be physically, mentally and emotionally very demanding, and in the case of the latter, extremely rewarding in terms of elation. But the challenge may not involve the spiritual centre, that most important aspect of being human.

If any performer can ignore the conventional and spurious aim of success and look beyond the ego, he or she can hope to find that special relationship with a particular environment. If the climber can feel at one with the rock, and the sailor, surfer or canoeist can be at one with the water, then this is potentially more deeply meaningful and more rewarding than egoistic 'success' – success as in the "… try to be a suck-cess" of Bob Dylan's play with this word in his singing of 'Subterranean Homesick Blues'.[52] The rewards are way beyond success. When this unity occurs it is a peak experience and, upon reflection, can be seen as a rejection of the feelings of separateness. Such experiences are uplifting. The fact that for most people the peak experience, or situation of 'deep flow',[53] is both rare and unpredictable is probably an indication of just how separate we have become. It is almost as if Nature were saying the following to human beings:

"As a member of the modern world you have separated yourself from my natural world in order to have an easier, more materialistic and self-centred lifestyle. If you wish to return to where you naturally belong, and you wish to understand the folly of your separateness, then you will find it difficult."

Devotion to an adventurous life needs to combine with trying to find that elusive harmony with a chosen environment. The relevance and meaning of the word beauty may not be particularly clear in this context, but I feel it is entirely appropriate. The *aim* of finding that harmony can be seen as a concept of beauty. The *action* involved in this process can have considerable beauty. In the most demanding adventures especially, efficient performance can only be achieved if the person is in a state of harmony with him – or herself. Physically, mentally and psychologically there needs to be that fine balance that expresses itself in the relaxed concentration that is the hallmark of the expert. In the best of these situations, the performer appears not only to make formidable difficulties look easy, but also seem to flow. Such apparent effortlessness, grace and rhythm are characteristics of harmony. Appropriately, this is only achieved after years of commitment and dedication, and in the final instance there is always the possibility of experiencing the joy of an elemental experience. Feelings of beauty, engendered by a sense of awe and wonder, characteristically describe these occasions.

In addition to beauty being used to describe personal actions, as an attitude to life it can also be seen as the essence of good relationships with other people. At one extreme, love between two people is obviously something of beauty. The same is true of a very close friendship. Those relationships, for example, forged in stress situations, not least in high adventure, can be both unforgettable and beautiful. Even fleeting moments between two strangers can sometimes be seen as beautiful moments in time. One early morning of a Pyrenean expedition found me on a col leading down to the head of a remote valley. I was in deep shadow and my mood matched the gloom. With a heavy pack, danger obviously lurked on the steep trackless slope beneath. To my amazement, I saw a figure coming diagonally up the slope, using a long wooden pole across his body for balance. When he reached me, he looked me in the eye, and then we spontaneously shook hands. The shepherd, in that single powerful grip and without words, seemed to say, "This is a magnificent wild place of which we are both a part". It was a moment of synchronicity and certainly of beauty.

Beyond human actions and relationships as a source of beauty, the word is in much more conventional usage when describing something experienced that is as uplifting as a glorious sunset or a profound work of art, which in itself may have been inspired by Nature. Indeed, there is so much beauty in the natural environment that it can be overwhelming. On the other hand, there may be times when, through familiarity, it is taken for granted, or even ignored. The only excuse I can see to ignore beauty is when there is preoccupation with survival situations. Even in these extreme occasions, flashes of beauty may occur. What I find particularly interesting is that somehow an awareness of beauty is enhanced after a dangerous experience. It is as if, having been close to 'going over the edge', one becomes much more aware of what it is to be alive in every sense.*

---

* Another example of experience in the post-adrenalin phase referred to in a footnote in 'Further Reflections'.

Receptivity can also be directly affected both by the situation you are in and how you arrived at that situation. If this statement is puzzling, let me give an example.

On my first Alaskan kayak trip with Barry Smith, I was acutely aware of the beauty of our surroundings. We returned from Sitka on a large ferry, which, at one point through the islands, covered the same seaway we had previously paddled. On the ferry, we had more time to admire the views. The same views, however, did not feel anything like as beautiful as when we had kayaked north.

There would seem to be two significant factors here, apart from the familiarity of the scene. The first was that on the ferry, unlike the kayaking, no physical effort – no physical connection – was involved. The second was that on the ferry we were completely cut off from the natural environment by glass canopies. There is a distinction between being in a wild place and looking at a view. Let me take this further with another example. The view from the top of a hill seems not to be the same if you have arrived through your own efforts, and through wild country, in comparison to being taken there, for example, by vehicle. The view is more likely to be better appreciated, in the former instance, because your self-reliant efforts have made you more aware. There seems to be wisdom here. The more effort you have to make, the more exposed you are to the influences of Nature and the greater the likelihood of being aware of its beauty. What this implies is that the greater the self-sufficiency and the fewer the barriers imposed by equipment and man-made features the greater the potential for heightened awareness. Being alone can further increase this awareness. These factors all point to the value of simplicity rather than complexity as an approach to life.

You have walked all day, steeply uphill. On top, you take off your boots and socks and place the soles of your feet on the bare ground. A moment of bliss? A moment of beauty? A realisation perhaps as to why the native Americans placed such importance on being in contact with Mother Earth.

The tiny flowers and the raindrop have as much beauty as the starry heavens, if they are truly seen. This recalls the classic words of William Blake:

"To see a world in a grain of sand
And heaven in a wild flower
Hold infinity in your hand
And eternity in an hour."[54]

The more beauty we see, the more we grow. There is beauty in *everything* in Nature, even if at times this gives us difficulties. I am referring here to what we perceive to be the cruel side of Nature. You may have already noticed that from a human perspective all the messages I have received from Nature have been very positive. They are the good news. If balance is a key aspect of Nature, then presumably there is also bad news. If this is not the case, then a critic could respond by saying Nature is unbalanced, or the author's viewpoint one-sided. I used the word 'presumably' because I do not feel there is bad news from Nature. One of the biggest problems facing Western cultures is their attitude to misfortunes, particularly to death. I do not have an entirely conventional outlook in this respect. I can remember reading a description of a fight to the death between two animals in the wild. What was so powerful in the writing was that the whole affair was seen as an event of beauty. If I had limited my response to empathy with the vanquished animal, perhaps beauty would have been the last thing on my mind; but then, my view would inevitably have been influenced by the human world and its sentiment.

It may be that in death, conscious self, the ego, has at last disappeared to be replaced by rejoining the unity of everything – a final act of serenity.

CHAPTER 11

INNER RESOURCES

W hat I have learnt from travelling in the wilderness has given me a deep inner sense of well-being when in the outdoors. My reflections on my experiences have taken me further along an inner journey towards understanding who I am and how I relate to my natural surroundings. It would be a delight if I could simply continue perpetually to be in the outdoors. But I cannot justify so extreme a lifestyle, despite its considerable attractions. To do so would be unacceptably selfish and self-centred. In addition to accepting that I am part of Nature, I must also accept that I am part of the human race. To accept this latter fact in a constructive sense means that I need to have a genuine concern for all humanity, in the same way that I have concern for the rest of the planet. To put this in another way, because I am not a hermit I have to accept a social contract: that as a member of human society I have obligations to that society, and that society has obligations to me. Is there anything I have learnt from my time in the wilderness then that might be of particular relevance and value to the man-made world?

My answer to my own question would be 'Yes'. Apart from feeling at one with Nature, being in and journeying through wilderness emphasises the need for positive rather than negative behaviour. Beneath the demands on mental and physical effort, on skill and on the emotions, lie the demands on inner resources. Well-being, and at times even survival, depend upon the presence of particular qualities. There is a wisdom here. Positive qualities or virtues are the means by which we travel towards well-being. Negative qualities or vices are the barriers. In all situations we have a choice: virtue or vice. In practice, humanity faces an unending battle between virtue and vice.* At times this may be depressing. On the other hand, and maybe this is inevitable, this conflict will show that one is alive and on a very meaningful journey.

As we make this journey through life, our actions will always reflect our inner strengths or weaknesses, our virtues or vices. This is why it is necessary

---

* Aristotle had a word for it – the psychomachia – the battle between good and evil in men's minds.

to carefully consider each action and ask whether we gave of our best. Only by such contemplation can we hope to progress towards inner contentment. This poses another immediate and difficult problem – the matter of deciding which qualities are the most worthwhile in terms of how one wishes to live. This needs careful justification.

I accept the fundamental right of every individual, within socially acceptable limits, to make their own choice of what they consider to be key qualities. This is a basic freedom. We live in a man-made world, however, where two associated problems seem relevant in this matter. The first is that the dominance of money and materialism can tend to encourage negative rather than positive qualities. The second is that this very freedom of millions of individuals, along with the complex range of qualities, can lead to confusion concerning which virtues are of particular importance. The laws of a modern society indicate the limits beyond which a person may not go without penalty, but these are negative boundaries. Thou shalt not steal, murder, exceed the speed limit, and so on. A more positive approach might be to work together towards an agreed group of virtues by which we should all try to live. Such an idea, of course, is as old as civilisation. Every religion, for example, directly or indirectly encourages and supports certain virtues. The fact remains that despite the strengths of religions and civilization, wars, chaos and planet devastation remain characteristic of human existence. It seems to me that with the increased ease of communication, it is not beyond human ability to reach a consensus of values which would accommodate the various creeds and cultures. It may also become essential if the human race is to survive.

In the 1970s, among old notes, I came across a list I had made of 70 virtues and vices. Further experience made me realise that a master list would probably be at least double that number. While there were overlaps, the large number was probably inevitable because of the considerable and complex range of human behaviour. For practical purposes, the original list was too long. It had to be radically reduced to become workable for purposes of reflection. By 1984 and the publication of *The Adventure Alternative*, I had selected seven virtues and their opposing vices. I'd now wish to extend this to ten. This group of positive and negative qualities I am presenting as particularly important have come from four main sources:

- looking through history at a range of outstanding and unusual people

- people I have met who have impressed me positively or negatively
- looking at my own strengths and weaknesses
- experiences in the wilderness.

It is, of course, a personal selection and is not put forward as a perfect master list. I do, however, feel confident that it is along the right lines in terms of possibly having universal application. This group of key virtues and opposing vices (see table) is proposed within a framework of values that accepts the implications of being both a member of the human race and of the planet.

Each virtue needs further explanation.

Honesty

"The most difficult thing in life is to live and not to lie – and not to believe in one's own lies."[55]

In a world where honesty's opposing vice of dishonesty is endemic, it has *elemental* importance. It may be helpful to view this virtue in three ways:

Honesty with oneself: To reflect upon one's thoughts, feelings and actions. To be aware that one can nearly always find reasons, or excuses, for all those occasions which do not reflect the best of oneself.

Honesty with others: To constantly appraise one's attitudes and actions concerning others. To try to be honest with kindness.

Honesty with the surrounding world: To try to accept the implications of the fact that one belongs to the unity of Nature.

Honesty may be seen as the foundation for all the other virtues. To act honestly is to act truthfully or conscientiously. Both truth and conscience are concerned with the human spirit. In the deepest sense, therefore, honesty would seem to be at the centre of being human. Emerson wrote, "truth is the summit of being".[56] If I ask myself, "What is truth?" I would reply that each of us is an inseparable part of Nature and our actions will not only affect ourselves but also our surroundings. It is essential, therefore, that we try to live honestly by virtues rather than vices. If we can do this,

Key virtues

HONESTY
It may be seen in three ways: honesty with oneself, with others and with one's surroundings. Conscientiousness, fairness and integrity are all characteristic of this virtue.

SELF DISCIPLINE
Being responsible for actions. Having the ability to control emotions and to resist desires and temptations.

DETERMINATION
Willpower, patience and hard work are key aspects.

SELF-RELIANCE
Self-confidence and self-respect based on an honest appraisal of one's experiences. Independence.

VITALITY
A positive approach to life with the characteristics of energy, enthusiasm, spontaneity and unremitting effort.

CREATIVITY
Being imaginative and perceptive, inventive and inspired.

UNSELFISHNESS
Being altruistic, friendly, kind and compassionate.

EMPATHY
The ability to project oneself with sensitivity into the object of contemplation, human or otherwise, and as far as possible without egoism.

HUMILITY
An unpretentious modesty which accepts that one is no more important than anyone else, regardless of one's abilities, power and status. Accepting that one is part of nature, and that, in terms of wisdom, the ego is unimportant. Accepting that the more one knows, the more there is to know.

COURAGE
A virtue of the spirit which can be expressed both physically and morally. In its finest sense it can be used to describe heroic commitment to a lifelong cause or a single act. Idealistically, it may be seen as an amalgam of the other nine virtues.

Key vices

DISHONESTY
Lying, deceit and hypocrisy.

INDISCIPLINE
Uncontrolled, impetuous and irresponsible behaviour.

IRRESOLUTION
Being weak-willed, passive and submissive.

DEPENDENCE
Unnecessary compliance and acquiescence.

APATHY
Lazy, indifferent and unresponsive.

DESTRUCTIVENESS
Harmful, pernicious and detrimental.

SELFISHNESS
Self-serving and self-seeking.

SELF-CENTREDNESS
Insensitive, conceited, egoistic and full of self-interest.

ARROGANCE
Self-important, egotistic, proud and contemptuous.

COWARDICE
Taking the easiest option. Faint-hearted and lacking spirit.

101

then we may eventually discover that truthfulness and honesty are synonymous with *integrity*. The ultimate meaning of integrity is concerned with the unity of everything.

Self-discipline

Self-discipline is an essential attribute for physical and mental health, for a satisfying yet consistent lifestyle and for responsible behaviour. Unfortunately, in an affluent and materialistic society especially, it is difficult not to be conditioned into always 'wanting' and 'having' rather than 'being'.[57] Desires can be strong and temptations lurk around every corner. I do not feel I am alone in finding an almost endless problem in this respect. Perhaps the wise person is one who needs the minimum of possessions, and who tries not to be dependent upon any of them.

In a broad context, the value of this virtue can be seen when one looks at the considerable extent of anti-social behaviour in our societies. Self-discipline, if practised on a much larger scale than at present, would considerably help to reduce this fundamental problem. Of all forms of discipline, external discipline is the worst, because it is imposed from *outside* the person.

In the world of adventure, self-discipline has a key role to play in the control of fear. The power of this emotion is well known. In extreme situations it can reduce a person to panic and can be very destructive. Even in less extreme situations, the deliberate choice of taking on a challenge that one knows is likely to stretch one's capabilities implies the necessity to control one's doubts and fears from the outset. Only the person in that situation has the power to exert self-discipline. The brain has to control the emotion.

Indiscipline, the opposing vice, would seem a trait to discourage. Uncontrolled, impetuous and irresponsible behaviour is largely, and for obvious reasons, self-damaging. There may well, however, be occasions when this is not true. To be present at a lecture, for example, where the speaker suddenly ignores the script and spontaneously expresses his or her emotions can be a worthwhile experience for both speaker and audience. *Always* to control the emotions could lead, in some circumstances, to self-discipline becoming a vice. Both inner growth and the development of relationships could suffer in that process and the faculties atrophy.

Determination

The number of synonyms for this quality indicates its importance. These include persistence, patience, resolution, industry, willpower, hard work, effort, perseverance, purposefulness, tenacity, endeavour, resolve and resilience.

Even a brief look at human achievement throughout history emphasises the obvious value of this quality. In the narrower world of adventure also, determination is obviously an essential for both survival and success. Like adventure itself, however, determination should not be seen completely in a positive light. It can be a vice, reflecting stubbornness, inflexibility and even ruthlessness. It can also demonstrate extreme selfishness and, sometimes, foolhardiness. This clearly indicates two points. The first is that the use of a quality, whether it is seen as a virtue or vice, is *situation specific*. The second is that a single virtue, and this is perhaps of particular importance with reference to determination, should not be viewed in isolation from other virtues.

At its extreme, as a virtue rather than vice, I suspect this quality has profound implications in terms of the journey inwards towards well-being. Throughout my life I have come across views that eternal truths can only come from experience of hardship and suffering. I hesitate to put a personal viewpoint because I stand in awe of those inspirational people who have been far down this arduous path. Nevertheless there have been times when my relatively minor experiences in the outdoors have strongly indicated that the way of hardship has been a major way to understanding self.

Self-reliance

William Blake captures its essence:

"No bird soars too high if he soars with his own wings".[58]

This composite quality appears to have two main constituents. The first of these, *self-confidence*, is one of the most worthwhile gifts that a person can possess, as it allows fears and doubts to be overcome. If it is to be a virtue rather than a vice, however, it must be linked to experience. As self-confidence grows, it allows a person to experience more, and this should be a lifelong process. If self-confidence, however, is not based on self-knowledge from experience, then it can become hollow and contemptible. The second constituent of self-reliance is the virtue of *self-respect*, which again is based on self-knowledge. This 'look in the mirror' quality implies the strongest of links with the virtue of honesty. It may also be seen as the foundation for dignity and ultimately of courage.

There is a natural logic in progression through life from total dependence as a baby to eventual independence or self-reliance. Independence of thought and action, regardless of popularity, are important characteristics of a mature person. This virtue, like determination, however, needs to be linked to other virtues. Honesty, for example, is essential. In the first instance there is a need to acknowledge that it is impossible to be completely self-reliant. We are all dependent on the planet for basic needs of water, food, air, light, warmth and shelter. In addition, unless we can live as hermits, we need relationships with other people. In other words dependency, the opposite of self-reliance, in some ways is not a vice. Interdependence – symbiosis to use the fashionable term – is a basic attribute of Nature.

Vitality

In an immediate sense, the meaning of vitality would seem obvious. Certain synonyms come to mind – enthusiasm, dynamism, energy and alertness. These are all qualities that could be ascribed to much of wild nature. Meeting people with vitality is always an impressive experience. It is akin to being suddenly in the presence of a gale. This type of vitality, however, is more like a gift, a personal attribute inextricably linked with charisma and considerable physical energy. It may not be appropriate, in this sense, to see it as a key virtue.

There is a deeper and more significant meaning to vitality, which is, or should be, relevant to everyone. This quality means facing up to the problems of life with enthusiasm, and in that process having a sharp awareness of the responsibilities of being a member of the human race and of the planet. I find it unsurprising that the philosopher Bertrand Russell regarded vitality as the most important of all the virtues. It is a virtue that has direct affinity with the 'energy' pillar of wisdom from Nature. It has an elemental value.

Vitality, in this deeper sense, is perhaps better understood by looking at the opposing vice of apathy. Kurt Hahn, the founder of Outward Bound, would seem to concur. In his view, apathy was the worst of human vices. At an individual level, there is, or should be, an unending battle within. "Do I give of my best, or not bother?" seems to be basic to being alive in the broadest of senses. The adolescent refrain of "Boring!" is one of the saddest sounds in the language.

Unselfishness

It is impossible to envisage a world without this virtue, which includes the qualities of compassion and generosity. Working on a mountain rescue team underlined its importance for me. Apart from the voluntary nature of the work and the team spirit, I was deeply impressed by the power of kindliness, friendliness and even humour to aid a person in serious trouble. Even a smile in a situation of stress can reduce tension and help someone else.

I prefer the term of 'altruism' to 'unselfishness', but the former seems to have fallen into disuse. Whichever term is used is unimportant. What matters is the use made of this virtue. Too often its use is restricted solely to concern for other human beings as a basis for action. This is too narrow a concept. It needs to be broadened to include the non-human world. If I walk down a footpath, for example, and a cobweb blocks my path, I should make the effort to avoid it. Whatever the situation, the unselfish act deliberately puts someone, or something else, before oneself in terms of importance. Commitment to this virtue would seem to be a major pathway to both inner contentment and to love in its deepest sense.

Empathy

Empathy is a word that can be easily misunderstood. Like unselfishness, it is a quality that requires one to move as far as is possible outside the importance of oneself, and then to try to understand the world, or situation, from that other standpoint. Its use is *not*, as may be commonly thought, restricted to relating to human beings. It is relevant to our relationship with *everything*.

I suspect that, in this latter sense, it can be a difficult virtue for many people to accept. If this is the case, I would emphasise that I intuitively feel this virtue is of profound importance when used in this regard to all our surroundings, animate and inanimate. My reasoning is as follows. We are conditioned to believe that we are separate from both other human beings and the environment, and the fact that we are part of both tends to be submerged. The use of empathy can break down these feelings of separation. Not only that, but it can lead ultimately to strong feelings of the unity of everything.

The more we can identify with what is around us, and especially with reference to the natural world, the more we can grow. To see the world from a viewpoint other than one's own can make a profound difference to understanding oneself. This remains true whatever the object of contemplation might be.

Empathy can also lead to a natural tendency to encourage other virtues rather than the self-centred vices.

Humility

Humility in its most profound sense seems difficult to define. Meeting people who possess deep humility is like seeing a cobalt sky after weeks of grey weather. In their presence, any thoughts of self-importance are likely to evaporate. The recent obituaries and reviews of the late Cardinal Basil Hume, for example, all agreed that humility was the essence of the man. Perhaps to possess a depth of this virtue is to be on the pathway to saintliness. One major way to develop it would be to try to avoid arrogance, its opposing vice. In practice that might present considerable challenges. Unless we have been singularly fortunate, from our earliest days we have been taught, consciously or otherwise, that the human race is superior to anything else in Nature. Even if our intellectual powers are greater than those of other life forms, I feel certain that we should try to avoid any feelings of superiority and keep man in perspective within the vastness of the universe. The unhappiness and anxiety among so many of the human race, and our increasing devastation of Nature, clearly indicates that our feelings of superiority are unacceptable.

In the modern world there is frequent opportunity for the individual to be arrogant rather than humble. The undue importance given to success encourages an aggressive outlook on life. I find it unsurprising that such societies produce leaders, in almost all walks of life, who tend towards arrogance rather than humility.

Creativity

The word 'creativity' has the same roots as 'creation' – from 'creare' (Latin) meaning to bring forth, to produce. The quality and well-being of society, to a large extent, may be defined by its degree of creativeness. Each human being has the potential to be creative, and almost every human activity has creative possibilities. There is obviously an urgent need to encourage this virtue at every opportunity, and to discourage its opposite of destructiveness whether in thought or deed. Each of us might benefit considerably if we reflected on our actions in terms of whether they were creative or destructive.

This virtue is, however, more profound than the immediate understanding of the word. Its source is the centre or spirit of the human being. Whilst it may develop from a range of factors, including experience in the chosen field, patience, determination, and even competition and stress, its spark comes from the deepest recesses of the unconscious. The moment of insight, intuition or inspiration typifies its origin. Such moments are intensely personal and can never be forced. It may even be that 'creativity' and 'spirituality' are intertwined, and in these moments, the conscious and unconscious merge, bringing feelings of considerable well-being and connection.

Courage

Beneath most acts of courage lies the shadow of fear that has to be overcome. Ignorance of the consequences of an action can reduce a possibly courageous act to one of markedly less value. The motivation for a courageous act is also of extreme importance. Such an act for reasons of personal gain, whether for materialistic or egocentric reasons, debases this noble virtue. Actions taken at the behest of the survival instinct are not necessarily courageous. Courage is the appropriate virtue to identify in any one who forgets wholly about themselves in their dedication to higher principles. Throughout history and in all forms of human endeavour there have been people who have exemplified this virtue. Similarly there have been many single acts of courage where people have risked everything in order to try to save others. Maybe the more appropriate word in this context is 'heroism'. It is heartening to find that, in a world where so much is a moral wasteland, courage of this type is still both revered and highly publicised. The media often tends to use 'courage' to describe extreme personal performances. This seems an inappropriate use of the word unless, for example, it pertains to recovery from traumatic or debilitating injury. 'Courage' should mainly be reserved for unselfish actions.

It may be helpful to see 'courage versus cowardice' as one of the recurrent themes in life, throughout which there are, or should be, unending opportunities to tackle this challenge. That process is likely to be both hard and sometimes frightening. But that is as it should be.

* * * * *

Some further comments need to be made about these key qualities.

In the original list I included the opposing vices, which reinforce the importance of the corresponding virtue. It may also be a wisdom as well as being a characteristic of being human that the vice needs to be experienced before one can fully appreciate the value of the corresponding virtue.

All ten virtues would seem to be important. They often overlap and should be regarded as interdependent. Some of these virtues, for example determination and self-reliance, if viewed in isolation and taken to extremes can become vices. The group should be seen as an entity. Only together can they become a harmony. Many famous human beings have, for example, markedly lacked humility, empathy and even honesty.

To demonstrate all ten virtues to a high degree would be to approach perfection. They are *ideals*. This should not stop us from trying to realise them. I suspect that each of us possesses the entire range of virtues and vices, even if we are unaware of many of them. Certainly if my own life is any guide, it was only later in life that I became aware that key qualities such as empathy, humility and creativity even existed within me. I had seen these virtues in other human beings when young but their importance to me only became meaningful when I reflected upon my own experiences. This seems to indicate that the development of virtues is a lifelong process.

The importance of these universal virtues, perhaps, is most evident when we look at human behaviour in extreme situations. I would like the reader to try and use the virtue of *empathy* in order to imagine the following situation.

Your name is Pete Goss … it is Christmas Day 1996. You are competing in a Solo Round the World Yacht Race and are in the Southern Ocean, 1200 miles south of Australia. There is a force nine gale blowing, with 50-foot following seas. You are very tense, if not frightened. The phone rings on your yacht. It is from Race Headquarters. A fellow competitor, the Frenchman Raphael Dinelli, has put out a Mayday call. Can you go to his assistance as you are nearest to him? The decision is obvious. Yes, you will go. The reality is horrendous as Dinelli is far behind you. You battle for two days against wind and sea to search the area, which is about the size of Hampshire, and quarter that area with no luck. As a last resort you stand by the mast, shouting and using a foghorn. Unbelievably, you spot his life raft. Dinelli is frozen and nearly dead. With great difficulty you get him into the tiny cockpit of your boat. He requires constant help, which you try to give as you sail to the nearest land. You finally arrive at Tasmania, 1800 miles to the north-east, put Dinelli ashore and then carry on with the race.[59]

Having tried to imagine the extreme challenge of such an experience, you may find it valuable to reflect upon it. In particular, apart from the immense physical, mental and emotional demands, many of the key virtues may seem to be of considerable relevance.

Unsurprisingly, Pete Goss was regarded as a hero in France, receiving the Legion d'Honneur, their premier award for gallantry. His heroic rescue of Dinelli is a superb example within the great traditions of adventure and rescue.

The whole area of adventure is fascinating in terms of the qualities displayed in stress situations. You may find it very worthwhile to look, for example, at the virtues of some of the early explorers of the oceans, great mountain ranges and polar regions, and compare them with some of the modern epics. I strongly suspect that some of the universal vices such as self-centredness, selfishness and arrogance tend to be much more prominent in recent times when commercial interests have become paramount.[60] The importance of money and status has sadly affected much adventure, as it has affected so many other aspects of human life. It is extremely important, however, to be wary about making judgements on the actions of other people. Quite apart from the impossibility of really knowing their motivations and how they saw a particular situation, one needs to accept that it is one's own motivations and actions that really matter.

There is a great tradition of human adventure and exploration, and in the final analysis it is not the successes or failures that are important. What are important, and are the bedrock of this tradition, are the virtues displayed by these explorers and adventurers. They have been my examples throughout life. Their elemental messages are there for all of us. Each of us needs to be aware, and especially when we feel low, that we all have huge potential with regard to all that is best about being human.

CHAPTER 12

A FRAMEWORK OF VALUES

I n the initial chapters, I put forward the straightforward notion that although we are all unique, we also share much that is common to the realm of human experience. We all have physical, mental and emotional aspects, and an ego that gives us a feeling of separateness from our surroundings. We all have a character that reflects our virtues and vices. We all have a spiritual centre that is the foundation of our values and humanity. We are also the same in that we are all part of Nature and have, beyond the contingent or the pathological, a common underlying goal in life in that we seek happiness and an enduring sense of well-being.

Subsequent chapters concentrated on an account of my own outer journey, then dealt with how I progressed along the inner journey towards a better understanding of myself and how I related to my natural surroundings. Of critical importance in that process were the elemental experiences. An understanding as to what they meant in terms of non-separateness led to a deep, inner contentment whenever I was in the wild. When I returned to the man-made world, however, that contentment disappeared and I wanted to return to my natural home as soon as possible. Instead of contentment I felt frustration.

A lifetime of working with people of all ages in adventure in the natural environment had convinced me of the great potential of being human in the best of senses, and not least in terms of holding to the virtues rather than the vices inherent in the human condition. The wilderness had shown me wisdom that led far down the road to personal happiness. Yet in the modern technological world, I was faced with very different external messages. Here is a sample.

- If it cannot be measured, it has no value.

- Image and presentation are important, not content.

- Bigger is better.

- Live now, pay later.

- Don't try and fix it – buy a new one.
- I'm alright, Jack.
- Make life as easy as possible.
- It's a weakness to say "Sorry".
- If there's a problem, ignore it or try to pass it on.
- One of the most important and popular pursuits in life is shopping.
- Instant everything.
- Cleverness is what really matters.
- Winning the lottery is the answer to our dreams.
- www.com is the only way to go.

Modern societies are so large and complex that inevitably there will be a bewildering variation of lifestyles and attitudes. Nevertheless, there do appear to be various worrying common features. My personal list would include the following:

- The increasing domination of the material in terms of what is important in life.
- The acceptance that aggressive competition is essential for success.
- The undue importance afforded to status and power.
- The accelerating trend towards a world of 'virtual reality' which is essentially impersonal and artificial.
- The tendency to use other people and the natural environment as resources for personal and immediate gain – in other words, as amenities.
- The fact that time is seldom allowed or spared for careful reflection.
- The increase in the number of controls and regulations in all aspects of living.
- The domination of vices rather than virtues.

- The emphasis by the media on bad news rather than good news, which encourages a pessimistic rather than optimistic view of human nature.

- Pollution of all kinds – physical, emotional and psychological.

- The importance of speed and convenience regardless of other considerations.

- The increasing glut of information, which can lead to confusion and the acceptance of superficiality.

- Undue and unnatural stress.

It gives me no pleasure to portray a gloomy view of the man-made world. Despite these comments, I am optimistic about the human race. In this troubled world there are many who can take pride in how they live. Throughout society virtues thrive. There are innumerable organisations and charities involved with aiding the less fortunate and concerned with protecting the natural world. The best side of human nature is revealed at all levels, from local to global.

The kindest of critics of the modern world, however, would accept that there are radical problems, and that the answers to these cannot be merely a matter of money. A simple example illustrates the point. The constant demand for more policemen, despite their already considerable numbers, clearly indicates problems with changes in human behaviour. A glance at the contents of a newspaper (local, national or international) also portrays a world not at ease with itself. There is tension everywhere. Human life seems beset by disagreements, confrontations and the never-ending topics of sleaze, crime, power, status or money.

My frustration with this world is directed, principally, at those who hold the power over human affairs.[61] As history clearly shows this power has always tended to reside in the hands of a small minority. The temptations to use this power for self-interest and unscrupulous ends have always been great. Nothing has changed in that respect. What has changed, however, is that modern technology and sophisticated communication systems have enabled global control by a minority of individuals and multi-national companies. If this small group, which is in effect a shadowy world govern-ment, had as its central aim the well-being of the human race and the planet, then the future might be bright. This seems not to be the case.

Global power seems ruthlessly intent on exploiting the rest of the human race and the planet. Its holders are sophisticated and unscrupulous. In the world of mass media hype, they not only have considerable control but also keep a low profile. Their power should never be underrated as they affect all aspects of modern life and even influence national governments. Their message is simple. Money is the god and with it comes power, the good life and ever increasing material benefits, regardless of the consequences.

If money *is* made the god, then the inevitable consequence is that it will encourage the worst aspects of being human, the vices rather than the virtues. I can remember as a schoolboy trying to hitch hike from the Midlands to north Wales and being on the side of the A5 road. The unrelenting flow of large lorries gave the strongest of impressions that I was in a world ruled by them. That event was nearly half a century ago. Now I feel that unless I escape to the natural world I am in distinct danger of being overwhelmed by the entire juggernaut of the materialistic world, which seems to go faster each year. I have – and no doubt share – a strong feeling of powerlessness in the face of many-faceted corruption and self-interest.

The temptation, if not the tendency, in modern life is to take from others and from one's surroundings what one feels is necessary for an enjoyable existence. Many people, of course, give as well as take, but I still feel the 'taking' is the predominant characteristic. An atmosphere is created in which what is seen to be important is the material well-being of the individual.

When put in a simple diagram, this realisation becomes even more poignant.

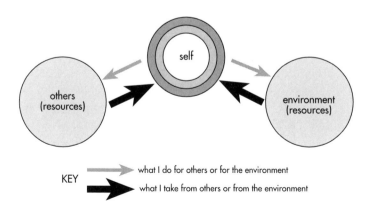

Such a diagram is, of course, a simplification. The size of the arrows, the amount of give and take, will depend upon the individual. The motivation for the action is also important. For example, I may take from my surroundings for altruistic or for egocentric reasons. I may do something worthwhile for others or for the environment because I genuinely care. Alternatively, my motivation may be for personal gain in some way or other. Human actions often stem from a mixture of both self-centred and unselfish motives.

What is important about this diagram, however, is that it shows three *separate* even though linked, entities. This is an illusory view. Such an approach to life treats other human beings and the planet as resources for personal benefit. This is precisely the approach of that small number of individuals and multinational companies that have the real power.

The central and underlying problem of the modern world is that it is built on the concept of separateness.

And yet, such foundations are built on sand. Governments can attempt to solve the many and complex problems within their societies, but they will fail unless they consider the underlying framework of society itself.

The separate circles shown in the previous diagram need to be replaced by a unity of circles.

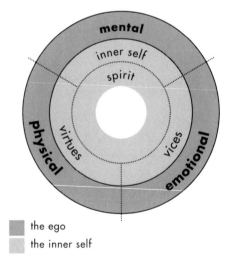

the ego
the inner self

Instead of other human beings and the environment being seen as separate resources, ideally they are part of self. By growing physically, mentally, emotionally and spiritually, then an individual would be reaching for the perfection of ideal self. Ultimately there would be an acceptance of the unity between everything.*

> *The central message from the wilderness is that there is a unity between everything in nature.*

Realisation of such unity may be idealistic and unsustainable, but it can be accepted as an ideal. Using this wisdom derived from wilderness experiences, therefore, I wish to suggest the framework of values to live by which I have used for many years and referred to in *The Adventure Alternative*. Such an idea may seem to impose on individual freedom. Yet I cannot ignore the realities of the modern world in which some individual freedoms may be bought at too high a social and environmental cost. The framework I am proposing is that, whatever our lifestyle, we try to accept the implications of the following principle. To live with:

an awareness of, respect for, and love of self

balanced with

an awareness of, respect for, and love of others

balanced with

an awareness of, respect for, and love of the environment.

By 'self' I mean in *all* senses, from physical, mental and emotional to, especially, the inner self. Although not directly mentioned, there is an implied balance within self between all these aspects.

By 'others', I am referring to the entire human race. Ideally this would include both previous and future human beings.

By 'environment', I mean the natural world and the man-made world.

The term 'balance' is crucial. Striving for balance is a central wisdom from nature. It is used in a sense of developing a harmony between the three elements involved in living: self, other human beings and the environment.

---

* See Appendix D.

The words 'awareness', 'respect' and 'love' are also of fundamental importance and progressively lead from one to another. The word 'awareness' is easy to write but extremely difficult to achieve and sustain. Awareness means 'pay close attention to': attention to what we see, hear, taste, smell or touch; attention to our actions and their consequences; attention to the details of living. Certainly, the more awareness I have in every sense, and in every situation, the more I can hope to understand. Whether positive feelings like respect or negative feelings like disrespect follow depends on what I value. If I behave badly in a situation, then I should feel disrespect for myself. Paradoxically, I may grow from this experience if I acknowledge my fault and am prepared to try to avoid it recurring. The more awareness and respect I have for myself, the more potential I have for positive growth.

When it comes to awareness and respect for other human beings, then major problems can occur. In terms of awareness, the virtue of *empathy* would seem essential. Only by trying to project oneself into the minds and situations of other people, beyond the barrier of one's ego, can one hope to begin fully to be aware of them and how they see the world. How much I can respect other human beings probably depends not just on my values, but also how I see myself. If I am honest, then I know that I am a mixture of strengths and weaknesses. In other words, when I look at others, I need to accept the same.* No one is perfect. I need to be positive, in that I should look at their strengths rather than only criticise their weaknesses. This can be extremely difficult within a competitive modern society.

Awareness and respect for the environment is perhaps easier to accept, at least in a shallow sense. Our surroundings provide us with the basic needs of air, water, food and shelter. The major thrust of conservation is understandably concerned with such issues. Common sense should dictate this need for respecting our environment. The different phases of my life as mountaineer and seafarer have carried the same message. I need as much awareness and respect for my selected environment as possible if I am to journey safely. This type of awareness, however, tends to be limited to a concern for physical well-being of humans. There are deeper levels.

Over a period of six months I walked up one hill, always the same way, many hundreds of times. This rather bizarre activity, for there were many

---

* The golden rule: do unto others as you would have done to yourself.

other hills around, was due to the steepness and length of this particular route. I was using it, with a full pack on my back, to train for expeditions. What I found interesting was that I did not become bored. I was nearly always finding or seeing something different on each ascent. As training progressed I came to know the intimate detail of the trail; the place of a rock or tiny plant. I came to love this particular hill because my awareness of it had greatly increased. I became concerned for its well-being and aware that the sheer volume, and often thoughtlessness, of people had increased erosion of it.

As our knowledge and experience of the interdependence of land, sea, sky and all the life forms of our planet increases, we can progress from the narrow focus on a specific location towards an awareness and respect for the whole complex universe.

My degree of awareness and respect at all levels, from the intimate to the planetary, greatly increased as a result of the high plateau experience in Alaska. Now, when I walk past a tree, for example, I try to be fully aware of it, and my respect for it is natural. I accept that not only is it another life form seeking its own well-being, but that it may well be 'looking' at me! It seems too arrogant to dismiss the possibility that it has some capability at least to sense what I am and what I feel. Such an apparently odd notion means that when I am alone in the wilds, I feel genuinely at home as I am surrounded by friends. I marvel at my feelings now, when for most of my life I was so self-centred, so unaware and so blind.

I have deliberately left the word 'love' until the last when looking at this framework. The importance of this word would seem to be profound. It is also very difficult to define clearly. The type of love I feel for the natural environment is what the Greeks termed *agape,* a universal love.* Whilst it may have taken most of my life to get to this stage with reference to, and reverence for, the whole of Nature, I suspect that, in essence, this kind of love is innate. The spontaneous actions and happy mood of young children when they are out of doors can be exhilarating to behold. They love it, and why not? They are natural. In the deepest sense, it is their home where they can instinctively play.

Even more revealing, perhaps, is the behaviour of many youngsters in a classroom when there is a gale blowing outside. It is common knowledge to

---

* There are other Greek meanings of the word 'love'. For example, 'eros' for the emotions of sensual desire, 'storge' for filial love and 'philos' for love shown to someone or something.

every teacher that they become excitable. My guess is that there is a simple, yet profound, reason for their unruly behaviour. They are expressing their unity with nature. That part of the child that is the wind has been switched on. *They are the wind!* The man-made classroom and the rules confine and restrict them. Instinctively they want the freedom to go everywhere.

At an adult level, millions of people through their experiences have developed a love of the environment or at least some aspect of it. The more intense their experiences, then the deeper that love is likely to be.* Of considerable relevance here is that key characteristic of nature, beauty. The recognition of beauty is very closely allied to the experience of love. They both are at the heart or centre of our existence. It may follow that the more beauty we recognise, the more love we may feel. Such an approach would diminish negative feelings concerned with apathy, ugliness and even hatred. It is not difficult to be inspired by those who have captured this love for the beauty of the natural environment. The subject has aroused creative passions since the dawn of human existence.

I know from my own experience as a young climber that although I loved the movement of climbing and the situations of steepness, there was an underlying fear of disaster. My love of the mountains, regardless of my situation within them, only came much later in life. In contrast, I suspect that one major reason I experienced a 'high plateau' on my solo Alaskan journey was that I immediately fell in love with that environment. I did not use that phrase at the time, and even now it sounds odd. There was no doubt, however, that I was awe inspired … such beauty on so vast scale, minimal trace of human beings and no pollution of any kind.

I have since come to realise that beauty and love are so important that, in one sense, life should be a search for them. The more beauty we can see then perhaps the more we have grown. Maybe there is beauty and ensuing love in everything, if we can but find it.

I acknowledge that love in the universal sense, amongst mankind, may well be the most important message that comes from human history. Looking at its opposite of hate and the mayhem caused by this vice underlines the point. This kind of love is the basis of many of the world's religions. The work of people like Gandhi, Mother Theresa, Martin Luther

---

• The only exception I can think of is in the case of people who have had such a traumatic adventure experience that they never revisit such environments. In these cases the power of fear may be greater than that of love.

King, Dag Hammarskjöld and countless others who have given so much of themselves for the love of their fellow human beings shows the importance of this deepest of feelings.

When I come to look at 'love of one's self', the matter is complicated yet again by what is meant by 'love' in this context. I do not, of course, mean love in a narcissistic sense. I see the word rather in terms of an 'ideal'. Within this ideal, perhaps self-respect, contentment and love are closely related. I was from an early age a discontented person. I was always reproving myself for my weaknesses. I still do this, but inwardly I have changed substantially. There is now a respect and love for that deepest part of me, and an underlying contentment. This can transcend my weaknesses and vulnerability. I know that this love has come from unremitting effort in the beauty of the wilderness. Gradually I have become more aware of my oneness with nature. I respect myself for my efforts. I also accept that the challenge is, and should be, endless.

BACK TO THE WILDERNESS

When I wrote *The Adventure Alternative* in 1984, over an intense three-month's sabbatical from my work, I vowed I would not repeat the experience. It had felt too much like an indoor expedition. Instead of the freedom of the outdoors, I had been confined to a desk. Whilst I enjoyed sharing ideas and experiences through lecturing, the lonely road of writing had given me little joy. Unsurprisingly, therefore, when I took early retirement in 1992, I spent as much time as possible on expeditions in the wilderness. I wanted to be far away from my desk, and from the rush of modern living and its education system.

In late 1997, I received an unexpected invitation to lecture in New Zealand. The delight of the opportunity to visit this country was tempered by the knowledge that I had no wish to fail my hosts. Reluctantly I returned to my desk to prepare the lecture. I was pleased and surprised that, although I had reflected little during my recent expeditions, as I had been too busy preparing and undertaking them, my thinking had moved on. Reading indicated, also, that what I had discovered was largely part of established wisdom. Whilst I was determined to share these ideas with the outdoor enthusiasts of New Zealand, my worry was that I knew, from experience, Kiwis were renowned for action rather than reflection. I presumed they would be much less enthusiastic about thoughts on an 'inner' journey. My fears proved groundless. The main lecture was warmly received and I then spent two months lecturing from Auckland to Dunedin.

I returned to England feeling I needed to put these ideas into a small book. This seemingly simple exercise proved nothing of the kind. As I struggled, often laboriously, through reams of paper, I realised increasingly that I had embarked on a dangerous journey. The nature of man, how he relates to his natural surroundings and what he can learn from that relationship is an intensely personal journey. Its deeper meanings were so profound that words seemed to be a highly inadequate tool. Nevertheless, I knew I had to persevere. The messages from the wilderness had left such indelible imprints on my psyche that I felt compelled to try to share them.

When I was a young man, I was silly enough to listen to a Cambridge graduate. "If you want to change society then the only way to do this is from within. Shouting from the outside is a waste of energy." A lifetime in state education has shown me clearly that radical change is not possible from within. I wonder now, however, if it was more a matter of unfortunate timing. The last ten years, at least, have seen a relentless tide of gross materialism sweeping over the modern world. Money has become the dominant factor – in education, in health, in sport and in almost every other walk of life. My impression, however, is that people are beginning to question what is going on and are turning slowly against this tide. My hope is that wisdom from the wilderness will increasingly find support. I want to believe that "there is nothing more powerful than an idea whose time has come".

As I return to wild places, and thankfully leave my desk, I ponder on what I have written and why I need to go back outdoors. The elements that make the outdoor journey seem so compelling are basic:

- a simple lifestyle
- surroundings of beauty
- an element of natural, rather than man-made, danger
- companionship
- spontaneity
- the *honesty* of the wilderness.

With these elements, an open mind and an open-hearted approach, I can find some contentment. I need to be true to my nature because, in essence, I am natural. I also wish to be with all my wilderness friends as I continue my search for wisdom. Alaska gave me that first oceanic feeling. I now seek …

"To be the flower
To bloom as the flower
And to enjoy the sunlight as well as the rainfall
When this is done, the flower speaks to me
I know all its secrets
all its joys
all its sufferings
That is – all its life vibrating in itself.
Not only that
Along with my knowledge of the flower
I know all the secrets of the universe
Which includes all the secrets of my own self."[62]

ENDNOTES

Frontispiece

(1) Merton, T. From the Introduction to *The Wisdom of the Desert, Sayings from the Desert Fathers of the Fourth Century*, translated by T. Merton. Hollis and Carter 1961

(2) From the *Katha Upanishad*. This version is used by P. Russell in his book *The Awakening Earth*. Ark Paperbacks 1985

See also: *The Ten Principal Upanishads*, translated by S.P. Swami and W.B. Yeats. Faber & Faber 1970, and *The Upanishads*, translated by J. Mascaró. Penguin 1973

Preface

(3) Thoreau, H. From the essay 'Walking', in *Works of Henry David Thoreau*, edited by L. Owens. Avenel 1981

(4) Marvell, A. From the poem 'To His Coy Mistress' (1681), in *The Complete Poems*, edited by E.S. Donno. Penguin 1972

Introduction

(5) Rousseau, J.J. "L'homme est né libre, et partout il est dans les fers." *Du Contrat Social* (1762), ch.1. Quoted in *The Oxford Dictionary of Quotations*. Oxford 1998

See also: *The Social Contract and Discourses*. Dutton & Dent 1950

(6) James, W. *The Varieties of Religious Experience*. Fontana 1975

(7) Hammarskjöld, D. *Markings*, translated by W.H. Auden and L. Sjöberg. Faber & Faber 1975

(8) Mortlock, C. *The Adventure Alternative*. Cicerone 1984

Chapter 1. Self

(9) Schopenhauer, A. *On Human Nature*, selected and translated by T.B. Saunders. Allen & Unwin 1926

(10) Roscoe, D.T. *Llanberis North, Climbing Guides to the Snowdon District*, edited by C.W.F. Noyce. The Climbers Club 1961

Chapter 3. The Impact of Other People

(11) Barker, R. *The Last Blue Mountain*. Chatto & Windus 1959

Chapter 4. The Impact of Nature

(12) Coles, K.A. *Heavy Weather Sailing*. John de Graff 1976

(13) Grading of rivers according to difficulty, *Guide to Waterways of British Isles*, edited and published by The British Canoe Union 1961

(14) Nietzsche, F. *Die Fröhliche Wissenschaft* (1882), bk.4, sect.283. Quoted in *The Oxford Dictionary of Quotations*. Oxford 1998

(15) Wordsworth, W. *The Prelude*. Book 1. Oxford 1969

Chapter 5. Sea Kayaking and Alaska

(16) Matthiessen, P. *The Snow Leopard*. Harvill 1996

(17) Muir, J. *The Wilderness World of John Muir*, edited by E.W. Teale. Houghton Mifflin 1954

Chapter 6. Elemental Experiences

(18) Jung, C.G. *Man and His Symbols*. Pan 1978

(19) Rumi, *Masnavi*, translated by W.E. Winfield. London 1898. Quoted in A. Huxley, *The Perennial Philosophy*. Chatto & Windus 1946

(20) For the editor, these words brought to mind Wordsworth's "Matthew" poems. Matthew, a Hawkshead schoolmaster, was revered and loved by William Wordsworth for his deep inner wisdom and joy of life – for his ability to 'be wilder'. Remembering a beautiful April morning, Wordsworth writes:

> Matthew is in his grave, yet now,
> Methinks, I see him stand,
> As at that moment, with a bough
> Of wilding in his hand.

Wordsworth, W. 'The Two April Mornings'. *Complete Poetical Works*.

www.everypoet.com/archive/poetry/William Wordsworth

(21) From the *Katha Upanishad*. This version is used by P. Russell in his book *The Awakening Earth*. Ark Paperbacks 1985

See also: *The Ten Principal Upanishads*, translated by S.P. Swami and W.B. Yeats. Faber & Faber 1970, and *The Upanishads*, translated by J. Mascaró. Penguin 1973

(22) Chuang Tzu. *Chuang Tzu, Taoist Philosopher and Mystic*, translated by H. Giles. Allen & Unwin 1961

(23) Traherne, T. *Thomas Traherne: Centuries, Poems and Thanksgivings, Volume 1*, edited by H.M. Margoliouth. Oxford 1972

(24) Bohm, D. *Wholeness and the Implicate Order*. Routledge 1995

Bohm then goes on to explain a hologram, where every part of an image is encoded in every part of the plate.

(25) Quoted in Naess, A. *Ecology, Community and Lifestyle*, translated and edited by D. Rothenberg. Cambridge 1989

(26) Murphy, M. and White, R.A. *The Psychic Side of Sports*. Addison-Wesley 1978

(27) Heinrich, B. *Mind of the Raven*. Harper Collins 1999. The behaviour, intelligence, and cultural texture associated with the raven are discussed at length in this book.

(28) Heinrich, B. *Ravens in Winter.* Summit Books 1989

(29) Happold, F.C. *Mysticism, A Study and an Anthology.* Pelican 1967

(30) *The Shorter Oxford Dictionary.* Oxford 1978

(31) Jung, C.G. *Synchronicity, An Acausal Connecting Principle.* Routledge & Kegan Paul 1987

(32) Maslow, A. *Religion, Values and Peak Experiences.* Ohio 1962

(33) Yanagi, S. *The Unknown Craftsman.* Kodansha 1972

(34) Happold, F.C. *Mysticism, A Study and an Anthology.* Pelican 1967

Chapter 9. A Pilgrim in the Wild

(35) Camus, A. *The Myth of Sisyphus.* Penguin 1975

This essay is particularly relevant in this context.

(36) Shakespeare, W. 'Hamlet' (1601), I. iv. 172. *The Complete Works of Shakespeare.* Harper Collins 1994

(37) Tomkins, P. and Bird, C. *The Secret Life of Plants.* Allen Lane 1973

(38) The Findhorn Community. *The Findhorn Garden.* Wildwood House 1976.

See also www.findhorn.org.

In 1962, Peter and Eileen Caddy and Dorothy Maclean came to live in the caravan park near the village of Findhorn, Morayshire. The gardens they made there in co-operation with nature attracted a lot of attention. People came to learn about the gardens and the principles behind them and from this the Findhorn Community developed.

(39) Whitman, W. From the poem 'Song of Myself', in *A Choice of Whitman's Verse,* selected by D. Hall. Faber 1987

(40) Muir, J. *The Wilderness World of John Muir,* edited by E.W. Teale. Houghton Mifflin 1954

(41) Thoreau, H. D. *Walden* (1854). 'Economy', in *Writings* (1906 ed.). Quoted in *The Oxford Dictionary of Quotations.* Oxford 1996

See also: Thoreau, H.D. *Walden.* Signet 1960

(42) Wordsworth, W. 'Lines composed a few miles above Tintern Abbey, on revisiting the banks of the Wye during a tour. July 13th. 1798'. *The Lyrical Ballads.* www.everypoet.com/archive/poetry/William Wordsworth

(43) Meister Eckhart. *Sermon LW XXIX.* The quotation is used by P. Russell in his book *The Awakening Earth.* Ark Paperbacks 1985

"All things are contained in the One, by virtue of the fact that it is one, for all multiplicity is one, and is one thing ... The One is not distinct from all things." A selected passage from www.geocities.com/Athens/9103/Meister Eckhart

See also: *The Internet Encyclopedia of Philosophy* www.utm.edu/research/iep/e/eckhart

(44) Suso, H. *Horologium Sapiente.* 1339. The British Library.

Henry Suso was a medieval mystic who worked with Meister Eckhart at Cologne after 1320. He also wrote the *Book of Divine Truth* in defence of Eckhart's teachings.

(45) Carpenter, E. *Towards Democracy*. George, Allen & Unwin 1918

Chapter 10. Seeking Unity with Nature

(46) Wolfe, T. *You Can't Go Home Again*. Heinemann 1947

(47) Keats, J. *Letters of John Keats*. Letter to George and Thomas, 21st December 1817, vol.1, edited by H.E. Rollins, 1958. See also the edition edited by R. Gittings, Oxford 1987

(48) Whitehead, A.N. *The Adventure of Ideas*. Cambridge 1939

(49) Lovelock, J.E. *Gaia, A New Look at Life on Earth*. Oxford 1979

(There are cogently expressed opposing views to this concept.)

(50) Keats, J. From the poem 'Ode to a Grecian Urn', in *The Complete Poems*, edited by J. Barnard, 2nd. edition. Penguin 1976

(51) Huntford, R. *Nansen*. Duckworth 1997

The quotation is taken from Nansen's diary for 1894.

(52) Dylan, B. 'Subterranean Homesick Blues'. © 1965; renewed 1993. Special Rider Music

(53) Csikszentmihalyi, M. *Beyond Boredom & Anxiety*. Jossey-Bass 1975

See also the same author's *Flow, The Psychology of Optimal Experience*, Harper Collins 1991

(54) Blake, W. 'Auguries of Innocence', in Blake, *Complete Writings*. Oxford 1979

Chapter 11. Inner Resources

(55) Huntford, R. *Nansen*. Duckworth 1997

Nansen used this quotation from Dostoevsky in a letter to his wife, Eva.

(56) Emerson, R.W. 'Character', *Essays: Second Series*. Allison no date, c.1900.

(57) Fromm, E. *To Have or To Be?* Abacus 1979

(58) Blake, W. From Proverbs of Hell, 'The Marriage of Heaven & Hell', in Blake, *Complete Writings*. Oxford 1979

(59) Goss, P. *Close to the Wind*. Headline 1998

(60) Krakauer, J. *Into Thin Air*. Macmillan 1997

Chapter 12. A Framework of Values

(61) Saul, J.R. *The Unconscious Civilization*. Penguin 1998

Epilogue

(62) Suzuki, D.T. *Studies in Zen Buddhism*. Rider 1955

BIBLIOGRAPHY

Abbey, E. *Desert Solitaire*. Ballantine 1981; *The Monkey Wrench Gang*. Canongate 1978

Allaby, M. *Thinking Green*. Barrie & Jenkins 1989

Bach, R. *Jonathan Livingstone Seagull*. Harper Collins 1994

Barker, R., *The Last Blue Mountain*.. Chatto & Windus 1959

Berry, W. *What Are People For*. Rider 1990

Blake, W. *Complete Writings*. Oxford 1979

Bohm, D. *Wholeness and the Implicate Order*. Routledge 1995

Bonington, C. *Quest for Adventure*. Hodder & Stoughton 1981

Bronowski, J. *The Identity of Man*. The Natural History Press 1971; *The Ascent of Man*.BBC Books 1981

Campbell, J. *The Power of Myth*. Doubleday 1989

Camus, A. *The Myth of Sisyphus*. Penguin 1975

Capra, F. *Uncommon Wisdom*. Century Hutchinson 1988

Carson, R. *Silent Spring*. Hamish Hamilton 1963

Chapman, F.S. *Watkins' Last Expedition*. Chatto & Windus 1931

Cherry-Garrard, A. *The Worst Journey in the World*. Constable 1922

Chinmoy, S. *Garden of the Soul*. Heath Communications 1994

Chuang Tzu. *Chuang Tzu, Taoist Philosopher and Mystic*, translated by H. Giles. Allen & Unwin 1961; *The Way of Chuang Tzu*, interpreted by Thomas Merton. Burns & Oates 1965; *Chuang Tsu, Inner Chapters*, translated by G. Feng and J. English. Wildwood House 1974

Clare, J. *The Shepherd's Calendar*, edited by E. Robinson and G. Summerfield. Oxford 1973

Coles, K.A. *Heavy Weather Sailing*. John de Graff 1976

Collister, R. *Over the Hills and Far Away*. The Ernest Press 1996

Cooper, J.C. *Taoism: The Way of the Mystic*. The Aquarian Press 1972

Csikszentmihalyi, M. *Beyond Boredom & Anxiety*. Jossey Bass 1975; *Flow: The Psychology of Optimal Experience*. Harper Collins 1991

Cupitt, D. *The Sea of Faith*. BBC Books 1984

Danziger, N. *Danziger's Britain*. Flamingo 1997

Daumal, R. *Mount Analogue*. Penguin 1974

De Saint-Exupery, A. *Wind, Sand and Stars*. Heinemann 1939

Dewey, J. *Democracy and Education*. Macmillan 1966

The Dhammapada: The Path of Perfection, translated by J. Mascaró. Penguin 1973

Dillard, A. *Pilgrim at Tinker Creek*. Pan 1976

Durckheim, K.G. *Absolute Living*. Arkana 1990; *The Way of Transformation*. Unwin Paperbacks 1988

Dylan, B. 'Subterranean Homesick Blues'. © 1965 renewed 1993. Special Rider Music

Emerson, R.W. *Selected Essays*, edited by L. Ziff. Penguin 1982

Findhorn Community. *The Findhorn Garden*. Wildwood House 1976

The Folio Golden Treasury, The Best Songs and Lyrical Poems in the English Language, chosen by J. Mitchie. Folio Society 1997

Fromm, E. *Man for Himself*. Routledge & Kegan Paul 1949; *To Have or To Be?* Abacus 1979

Gibran, K. *The Prophet*. Heinemann 1980

Gill, E. *A Holy Tradition of Working*. Golgonooza Press 1983

Giono, J. *The Man Who Planted Trees*. Peter Owen 1954

Golman, D. *Emotional Intelligence*. Bloomsbury 1996

Goss, P. *Close to the Wind*. Headline 1998

Guide to Waterways of British Isles, edited and published by The British Canoe Union. 1961

Gurdjieff, G.I. *All and Everything*. Routledge & Kegan Paul 1949

Halpern, D. *Antaeus on Nature.* Collins Harvill 1989

Hammarskjöld, D. *Markings,* translated by W.H. Auden & L. Sjöberg. Faber & Faber 1975

Happold, F.C. *Mysticism, A Study and an Anthology.* Pelican 1967

Harding, D.E. *On Having No Head.* Arkana 1986

Harvey, A. *A Journey in Ladakh.* Jonathan Cape 1983

Heinrich, B. *Ravens in Winter.* Summit Books 1989; *Mind of the Raven.* Harper Collins 1999

Hodgkin, R.A. *Born Curious.* John Wiley 1976

Hopkins, G.M. *A Selection of his Poems and Prose,* edited by W.H. Gardner. Penguin 1963

Humphreys, C. *Zen Buddhism.* Heinemann 1971

Hunt, J. *In Search of Adventure.* Talbot Adair 1990

Huntford, R. *Nansen.* Duckworth 1997

Huxley, A. *The Perennial Philosophy.* Chatto & Windus 1946

Huxley, E. *Scott of the Antarctic.* Pan 1979

The Internet Encyclopedia of Philosophy at www.utm.edu/research/iep/e/eckhart

James, W. *The Varieties of Religious Experience.* Fontana 1975

Jefferies, R. *The Story of My Heart.* Longmans, Green & Co. 1922

Jung, C.G. *Man and His Symbols.* Pan 1978; *Synchronicity, An Acausal Connecting Principle.* Routledge & Kegan Paul 1987

Junger, S. *The Perfect Storm.* Fourth Estate 1997

Keats, J. *Letters of John Keats,* edited by R. Gittings. Oxford 1987; *The Complete Poems,* edited by J. Barnard. 2nd Edition. Penguin 1976

Kennedy, J.F. *Profiles of Courage.* Memorial Edition, Harper & Row 1964

Kierkegaard, S. *Fear & Trembling, & Sickness Unto Death.* Princeton 1974

King, H. *South Pole Odyssey.* Blandford 1982

Koestler, A. *Arrow in the Blue.* Collins 1952

Krakauer, J. *Into Thin Air.* Macmillan 1997; *Into the Wild.* Macmillan 1998

Laski, M. *Ecstasy: A Study of Some Secular and Religious Experiences.* Indiana 1962

Leach, B. *Drawings, Verse & Belief.* Jupiter 1977

Leopold, A. *A Sand County Almanac.* Oxford 1981

Lopez, B. *Arctic Dreams.* Picador 1987; *About This Life.* Harvill 1998

Lovelock, J.E. *Gaia A New Look at Life on Earth.* Oxford 1979; *The Ages of Gaia.* Oxford 1989

Lowe, B. *The Beauty of Sport.* Prentice Hall 1977

Maslow, A. *Religion, Values & Peak Experiences.* Ohio 1962; *Motivation & Personality.* Harper & Row 1970

Matthiessen, P. *The Snow Leopard.* Harvill 1996

Meister Eckhart. *Sermon LW XXIX* at www.geocities.com/Athens/9103/Meister Eckhart

Merton, T. *Elected Silence.* Burns & Oats 1961

Moittoissier, B. *The Long Way.* Adlard Coles 1974

Mortlock, C. *The Adventure Alternative.* Cicerone 1984

Muir, J. *The Wilderness World of John Muir,* edited by E.W. Teale. Houghton Mifflin 1954

Murphy, M. and White, R.A. *The Psychic Side of Sports.* Addison-Wesley 1978

Naess, A. *Ecology, Community and Lifestyle,* translated and edited by D. Rothenberg. Cambridge 1989

Niebuhr, R. *The Nature and Destiny of Man.* Scribner's 1949

Noyce, C.W.F. *They Survived.* Heinemann 1962

The Oxford Dictionary of Quotations. Oxford 1998

Paffard, M. *Inglorious Wordsworths.* Hodder & Stoughton 1973

Passmore, J. *Man's Responsibility for Nature.* Duckworth 1980

Pedlar, K. *The Quest for Gaia.* Granada 1981

Perrin, J. *Visions of Snowdonia.* BBC Books 1997; *Spirits of Place.* Gomer 1997; *River Map.* Gomer 2001

Pilger, J. *Hidden Agenda.* Random House 1998

Porter, E. *In Wildness is the Preservation of the World.* Sierra Club 1971

Raine, K. *Defending Ancient Springs*. Golgonooza Press 1985; *Living With Mystery*. Golgonooza Press 1992; *The Presence*. Golgonooza Press 1994

Ralling, C. *Shackleton*. BBC Books 1983

Riddell, C. *The Findhorn Community*. Findhorn 1991

Rohe, F. *The Zen of Running*. Random House 1975

Roscoe, D.T. *Llanberis North, Climbing Guides to the Snowdon District*, edited by C.W.F. Noyce. Climbers Club 1961

Roszak, T. *Person/Planet*. Anchor 1978

Russell, B. *The Conquest of Happiness*. Allen & Unwin 1930; *Education and the Good Life*. H. Liveright 1954; *The History of Western Philosophy*. G. Allen & Unwin 1971

Russell, Peter. *The Awakening Earth*, Ark Paperbacks 1985

Sagan, Carl. *The Dragons of Eden*. Random House 1977

Saul, J.R. *The Unconscious Civilization*. Penguin 1998

Schopenhauer, A. *On Human Nature*, selected and translated by T.B. Saunders Allen & Unwin 1926

Schumacher, E. *Small is Beautiful*. Sphere Books 1973

Schweitzer, A. *My Life and Thoughts*, translated by C.T. Campion. Allen & Unwin 1933

The Secret of the Golden Flower, translated by R. Wilhelm & C.G. Jung. Routledge & Kegan Paul 1972

Shakespeare, W. *The Complete Works of Shakespeare*. Harper Collins 1994

Shepherd, N. 'The Living Mountains', in *The Grampian Quartet*. Canongate 1996

Shipton, E. *The Six Mountain Travel Books*, edited by J. Perrin. Diadem Books 1985

The Shorter Oxford Dictionary. Oxford 1978

Smythe, F.S. *The Spirit of the Hills*. Hodder & Stoughton 1940

Solomon, R.C. *From Hegel to Existentialism*. Oxford 1987

Solzhenitsyn, A. *Alexander Solzhenitsyn Speaks to the West*. Bodley Head 1978

Suso, Henry. *Horologium Sapiente*. 1339. The British Library

Suzuki, D.T. *Studies in Zen Buddhism*. Rider 1955

Taplin, K. *Tongues in Trees: Studies in Literature and Ecology*. Green Books 1989

The Ten Principal Upanishads, translated by S.P. Swami and W.B. Yeats. Faber & Faber 1970

Thoreau, H.D. *Works of Henry David Thoreau*, edited by L. Owens. Avenel 1981; *Walden*. Signet 1960

Toffler, A. *Future Shock*. Pan 1970

Tomkins, P. and Bird, C. *The Secret Life of Plants*. Allen Lane 1973

Touch the Earth, A Self Portrait of Indian Existence, edited by T.C. McLuhan. Abacus 1973

Traherne, T. *Thomas Traherne: Centuries, Poems and Thanksgivings*, edited by H.M. Margoliouth Oxford 1972

Trungpa, C. *Cutting Through Spiritual Materialism*. Shambhala 1987

The Upanishads, translated by J. Mascaró. Penguin 1973

Van der Post, L. *A Walk with a White Bushman*. Penguin 1988

Watson, L. *Lifetide*. Hodder & Stoughton 1979

Watts, A. *Cloud Hidden, Whereabouts Unknown*. Sphere 1977

Whitehead, A.N. *The Adventure of Ideas*. Cambridge 1939

Whitman, W. *A Choice of Whitman's Verse*, selected by D. Hall. Faber 1987

Wilbur, K. *A Brief History of Everything*. Gill & Macmillan 1995

The Wisdom of the Desert, Sayings from the Desert Fathers of the Fourth Century, translated and introduced by T. Merton. Hollis and Carter 1961

Wolfe, T. *You Can't Go Home Again*. Heinemann 1947

Wordsworth, W. *The Prelude*. Oxford 1969

The Complete Poetical Works at www.everypoet.com/archive/poetry/WilliamWordsworth

Wyatt, J. *The Shining Levels*. Penguin 1973

Yanagi, S. *The Unknown Craftsman*. Kodansha 1972

Young, G.W. *On High Hills*. Methuen 1927 Bœ

APPENDIX A

BASIC BELIEFS

The following beliefs form an essential background to the ideas within this book.

Life is a journey, but for most Westerners the most challenging aspect of it may well be the journey inwards. This presupposes extensive journeys having been made outwards! The more demanding the outward journey, the more potential for inward reflection. Both journeys are potentially synonymous.

Quality action and quality reflection on that action are of fundamental and equal importance.

Life is, in its most fruitful and fulfilling mode, a search for ideals of beauty, wisdom, happiness, love, freedom and unity.

Whatever life is about, it must surely include the aim of maximum development of the whole potential of an individual. This not only includes the physical, mental and emotional aspects of personality, but also a search for and implementation of a personal framework of values.

Education in its broadest sense means learning about life. This is a lifelong process and a search for fulfilment. It includes trying to understand who we are and how we relate to everything around us.

Each of us is an inhabitant of this planet and therefore a part of Nature. We have obligations, therefore, to the Earth.

As far as possible the natural environment and everything within it should be regarded as sacred. The human race should regard it with maximum awareness, respect and love. This implies minimal disturbance, pollution and damage. To use the natural as a resource purely for human-centred gain is to stunt human well-being. The needs of the planet are the needs of the person. We need proper reverence for the sanctity of the earth. Actions against the planet are actions against ourselves.

Each of us is a member of society. So we have obligations to that society, and that society has obligations to us.

Modern societies are excessively materialistic, with a 'live now, pay later' approach to life. They tend to be dominated by negative qualities such as selfishness, deceit, arrogance and greed. Much of the planet has been polluted or destroyed. The future of the world may well depend upon the human race learning to live, work and play together within an agreed framework of values. A radical change in modern lifestyle is necessary, from a way of 'having' to a way of 'being'".

No human being is more or less important than any other human being.

No human being is more or less important than anything else in Nature. For human beings to regard themselves as in anyway superior to anything else in Nature is to take a stance of arrogance rather than of humility.

More than anything else, including our accomplishments, our behaviour determines our quality as a human being.

The answers to life are concerned with simplicity not complexity. If this is a perennial wisdom, it follows that modern societies are increasingly being led in the wrong direction. Complexity, not simplicity, is a major characteristic of the modern world.

To adventure in the natural environment often means to face challenges at or near the edge of our capabilities in as self-reliant a manner as possible. The more natural – as distinct from contrived – and simple the journey, the more potential for personal growth.

The more we grow, in all senses, the more beauty we can see, both within and around us. A key to happiness may lie in the search for beauty.

APPENDIX B

OUTDOOR EDUCATION

Bearing in mind the problems of living in the modern world and the urgent need for a framework of values within societies, the natural environment should be core curriculum. Young people can then learn about the environment, about how to protect it and about their relationship with it. They can also realise their own potential there in the fundamental sense of being human.

Outdoor Education urgently needs:

- an overall concept or framework that accepts humanity is at least part of Nature and not separate from it
- an ability to speak with one powerful voice as to why modern societies and their educational systems need to radically change direction from 'having' to 'being'.

Young people are the most important resource in the human world. Like acorns they have the potential to become giant oak trees. Formal education, at best, tends only to begin to develop this potential. All of us have potential far beyond our imaginations.

I believe the urge to explore, to find out, to adventure is instinctive. Failure to provide socially acceptable outlets for this instinct may both stunt personal growth and the progress of any modern society. Much of antisocial and criminal behaviour by young people may be attributed to this need for challenge and excitement.

In terms of personal growth, almost all young people can benefit from adventure and expeditions. Such journeys should eventually be as self-reliant as possible.

Young people tend to have a natural affinity with the outdoors. They are often easily enthused both to explore and care for Nature.

The first responsibility of any outdoor instructor is to give those in his or her care a sense of awe and wonder of all that surrounds them in a natural environment, and a sense of their own potential. Philosophy, the love of wisdom, begins in wonder.

The outdoor instructor or teacher should be an ambassador for the natural environment.

APPENDIX C

FUTHER NOTES ON INNER RESOURCES

With reference to virtues and vices being bi-polar

For the purpose of discussion, the distinction between opposing traits has been that they are bi-polar, from extreme positive to extreme negative. However, I accept ultimately the wisdom of the paradox that truth is where opposites meet. This idea is beyond my ability to explain rationally but should not be disregarded because of this problem. I feel the language of analysis invites divisions that may not exist, and focusing on the parts loses sight of the whole.

The development of virtues

Three further inner resources not included in the main text seem particularly worthy of attention: humour, concentration and commonsense.

Humour

There can be little doubt that this is, or can be, a key virtue. Indeed the more serious the situation, then the more likely the need for humour to relieve the stress. I vividly remember the years working on the Langdale/Ambleside Mountain Rescue Team. In some grim situations it was humbling to see humour used to very positive effect with the casualties. This example also seems to illustrate something unusual about this virtue. Unlike most of the ten virtues in the text, its opposite of 'seriousness' is not, or need not be, a 'vice'. In other words, here is a situation where both poles of the trait, extreme humour and extreme seriousness, can be involved in a very positive manner.

Humour is not mentioned in the list of universal virtues, not because it is unimportant but because I see it as a part of vitality and, at times, of courage. It may also have links with other virtues such as empathy and unselfishness. And it provides a leavening perspective.

Concentration

Concentration is obviously of considerable importance, and perhaps should be regarded as an essential attribute rather than a virtue. My impression is that the whole issue of concentration is complex and far too readily dismissed as easily understood. At one level it can been seen as an aspect of our mental faculties. Concentration is often listed as a key component of efficient thinking. At another level, I suspect that complete concentration is no less than the whole of the person being involved in the task at hand. This type of concentration is often extremely difficult to achieve and in some situations may take years to perfect. A key element in these situations is relaxation! In other words, I am suggesting that complete concentration is 'relaxed concentration'. Whilst this may sound paradoxical, perhaps the phrase becomes more meaningful if I bring in the opposite of 'relaxed' which is 'tense'. Even the slightest degree of tenseness, conscious or unconscious, will prevent complete concentration, as it will interrupt the flow or harmony of total involvement.

Having some experience of yoga, I can see that meditation, the end state of the activity, can only be achieved by complete relaxation. Again, such relaxation can be very difficult to achieve. I find it intriguing that in the *Penguin Dictionary of Synonyms and Antonyms* (Penguin 1992), 'meditation' is a synonym for 'concentration'!

There are some situations where relaxed concentration would not appear to be relevant. In an emergency for example, where sudden danger threatens, the human being can act in a 'blink of an eye'. What seems to happen here is that bodily mechanisms take control instinctively. In that split second, concentration is absolute but you have not even had time to think about it.

Commonsense

The matter of commonsense sometimes arises in discussions on the key virtues. I suspect strongly that this, too, is an attribute rather than a virtue. This is not to deny its considerable importance – which can clearly be seen where there is a lack of it. On some occasions when I have not used my commonsense, I have been lucky to survive. I would regard a high adventure threshold and a marked lack of commonsense as a potentially lethal combination. Perhaps commonsense is a combination of experience allied to some inbuilt or intuitive faculty.

It is taken for granted that physical, technical and intellectual skills are developed through progressive practice. I feel the same is true of virtues. They may develop and strengthen through constant and ideally progressive use. It may also be that a difficult and challenging lifestyle will tend to promote the virtues, if the individual has a clear idea of their own framework of values.

APPENDIX D

INNER SELF AND IDEAL SELF

I have always felt that if I could draw an idea or concept, it would help my understanding of it. There seems to be considerable significance in circles. It was almost a moment of synchronicity to discover Jung's mandalas. Apparently 'mandala' is Sanskrit for 'circle', and Jung had no doubt of their profound importance. Circles seem to me both fundamental aspects of Nature, for example, the sun and the earth, and also to express a profound truth in that ultimately there is no beginning and no end.

Some of the basic aspects of being human are expressed in the following mandala.

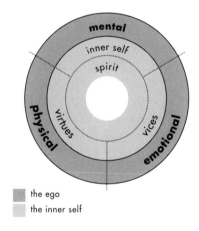

■ the ego
■ the inner self

Inner self

The extent and relative proportions of each circle will vary according to the individual and situation.

- The most important aspect of being human is the spirit or centre.
- The spiritual centre is the home of our beliefs and values.
- Love and happiness, in their deepest senses, lie within the spiritual.

Ideal self

Instead of other human beings and the environment being seen as separate from self, ideally they are seen as part of self.

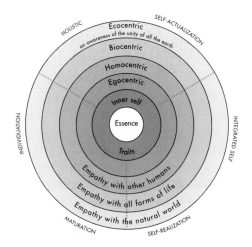

The circles outside of the inner self refer to the individual's approach to life and their consequent lifestyle.

Ideal self, as shown in the outer circle of the diagram, is the maximum development of self.

Different terms have been used to describe this perfection:

- ideal or holistic self
- maturation
- individuation (from Carl Jung)
- integration of the personality (from A. Storr)
- self-actualization (from A. Maslow)
- self-realization (from Arne Naess).

You can ask, "Where am I within these circles?" In other words, "What is my attitude to life?" or, "Is my view of life essentially egocentric, homocentric, biocentric or ecocentric?" In all likelihood, different situations will mean variations in one's approach to life. For example, in an immature moment I may act in an egocentric manner. In another situation, I may react in an ecocentric way. Nevertheless, as one grows, hopefully one is likely to adopt one of the more constructive and altruistic approaches to life.

COLIN MORTLOCK

C olin Mortlock was born in 1936 and educated at Bemrose Grammar School, Derby, and Keble College, Oxford, where he graduated in Modern History. A keen athlete, he went on to Loughborough College to take first class honours in Physical Education and Education.

After teaching at the Royal Wolverhampton School and Manchester Grammar School he became, in 1965, Warden of The Woodlands Outdoor Centre in south Wales. This centre for school children from the city of Oxford soon became recognised as one of the country's leading adventure centres. In 1971 he was appointed Director of the Centre for Outdoor Education, Charlotte Mason College, Ambleside, in the Lake District. Over the next twenty years the Centre became renowned both for its degree courses and especially for its one-year International Adventure course for experienced teachers.

Apart from a lifetime in Outdoor Education, Colin has acquired a considerable reputation for his own adventures. In the 1960s he was one of Britain's top rock climbers, and was probably the first to devise and use a climbing wall. He led an Oxford Expedition to Norway and was on the successful Trivor Himalayan Expedition. He later went on to discover Pembrokeshire sea-cliff climbing and wrote the initial guidebook. After several years of white-water canoeing and small-boat sailing off the west coast of Britain he began sea kayaking. In 1975, he was awarded a Churchill Scholarship for leading a pioneering six-man kayak expedition along the arctic coastline of Norway and round the North Cape. This was followed in 1979 by a two-man kayak expedition along the Alaskan coastline from Prince Rupert to Sitka. In 1981 he returned to Sitka and made a 650-mile solo kayak journey to the north, including Glacier Bay. In the following years he spent a considerable time establishing and working as Chairman for the Ambleside and Area Adventure Association and the Lakes Community Outdoor Project. Together these charities provided outdoor experiences and sports resources for the local community. He returned to the mountains of Europe in 1988, and since retirement in 1991 has covered over 15,000 miles trekking in the wild, often alone.

Colin Mortlock was founder and first chairman of the National Association of Outdoor Adventure Education. He is currently chairman of the Adventure & Environmental Awareness Group. He has written extensively on outdoor education and has an international reputation as a keynote lecturer on adventure and values. His other book, *The Adventure Alternative*, was published by Cicerone in 1984 and remains in print.

Colin lives in the English Lake District with his wife, Annette, and has three grown-up daughters.

COMMENTS ABOUT *BEYOND ADVENTURE*

Beyond Adventure is an extraordinary autobiography. A book to be read and pondered over by anyone for whom mountain, river or sea is more than an outdoor gymnasium.

Rob Collister, Mountain Guide and Author

This book deserves to be an historical document, although it is not a book about history. It deserves to be read and studied by academics, although this is not an academic book.

Steve Bowles, Humanistic Polytechnic, Tornio, Finland

I enjoyed it very much, and although I cannot claim to have had experiences even close to the ones you describe, I feel that everything that you say rings incredibly true.

Mike Ross, Writer

Anyone who considers it worthwhile to reflect upon the human condition, social interaction or the relationship of our species to environment will find much to engage them.

Jeremy Roxbee Cox, *Environmental Values*, IEPP, Lancaster University

Beyond Adventure is a fascinating rendition of philosophical and soul-searching ideas that come from the depths of his personal adventure experiences. It is a book that should grace the shelves of universities, other libraries and the homes of all outdoor enthusiasts.

Ray Goldring, Outdoor Instructor and Outdoor Safety Consultant, New Zealand

Very original and very Colin!

Doug Scott, Mountaineer and Author

It is the tale of the Ancient Mariner and has something of his earnestness.

A review cannot do justice to a book that tries to probe as deeply as this. It can only prompt the arguments and alternatives, the dissentions and recognitions that ought to follow it.

The antidote to Joe Simpson.

Terry Gifford, *High* magazine

Beyond Adventure has now joined *Marcus Aurelius* and *Sand County Almanac* beside my bed. What you say is so important for every living being, I hope it gains the recognition it merits.

Margaret Ellis, Archaeologist and Teacher of English

I found it fascinating reading. Anyone who meets Nature close to, or anyone who longs to, should read it.

Norman Frith, Architect and Quaker

Beyond Adventure is essentially a deeply thoughtful exploration of motives and relationships, virtues and values. It is a book to savour slowly, to ponder over, to endow excursions into the great outdoors with a new perspective.

George Bott, *The Keswick Reminder*, March 15th 2002

One of the most inspirational books I've read on the outdoors. It deserves to be read widely. May its theme be taken up by all who hear the Call of the Wild.

Kev Reynolds, Author, Photojournalist and Lecturer

The openness and honesty of *Beyond Adventure* for me reveals genuine bravery born of a deeper wisdom. This is an important book for our times.

Jeremy Wilson, Environmentalist and Farmer, Friluftsliv Movement in Norway

I've just read and been engaged by *Beyond Adventure,* finding much in accordance with my own experience although my background is somewhat opposite.

Roger Whitfield, Craftsman and Photographer

There is a very great deal in this thought-provoking book. It will be relished by anyone with a love of adventure in the natural world and particularly those who feel a commitment to its conservation.

John Wyatt, *Magazine of Friends of the Lake District* No. 39, 2002

Insightful; it opened my eyes and mind.

It goes beyond my self-imposed boundaries.

A journey to the inner self. This book should be on every outdoorsman's shelf.

Submitted by **Eric (Spider) Penman,** Climber and Outdoor Instructor

A little like reading *Jonathan Livingstone Seagull*.

Beyond Adventure takes the reader a stage further in his understanding of the human being and its potential for oneness with nature and the environment.

Nigel Williams, *The Leader*, British Association of European Mountain Leaders

This book explores the deeper reasons for wanting to head outdoors in order to seek adventure. Well worth a read, because it describes the feelings that can easily be missed in the busy lives that so many people lead.

Mike Dales, *Scottish Mountaineer*

Beyond Adventure...Beyond Classification!
The nature of your book ensures that anyone browsing in this library could find it amongst the environment, philosophy or outdoor sections.

Jackie Fay, Librarian

It makes for a challenging read. His arguments were so passionate and so thoroughly backed up by reference to his litany of intense experiences that it would be pointless dismissing them as ravings. Instead they demand serious reflection from any individual active in the great outdoors.

Mike Dagley, Mountaineering Council of Ireland, *Irish Mountain Log 61*, Spring 2002

I loved your book for what it said to me, for these were words about my very own relationship with nature.

Neil Allinson, Mountain Guide

Mortlock is passing on messages that a lifetime of wilderness adventuring have imprinted on his psyche. Translating a set of personal truths evolved over years of inner searching into a framework of values for the rest of us might seem presumptuous. Yet it is managed with utmost humility.

Stephen Goodwin, *Climber*, March 2002

Allow it to stretch your imagination too.

Cameron McNeish – *TGO (The Great Outdoors)*, December 2001

LISTING OF CICERONE GUIDES

NORTHERN ENGLAND
LONG DISTANCE TRAILS
- THE DALES WAY
- THE ISLE OF MAN COASTAL PATH
- THE PENNINE WAY
- THE ALTERNATIVE COAST TO COAST
- NORTHERN COAST-TO-COAST WALK
- THE RELATIVE HILLS OF BRITAIN
- MOUNTAINS ENGLAND & WALES
  VOL 1 WALES
  VOL 2 ENGLAND

CYCLING
- BORDER COUNTRY BIKE ROUTES
- THE CHESHIRE CYCLE WAY
- THE CUMBRIA CYCLE WAY
- THE DANUBE CYCLE WAY
- LANDS END TO JOHN O'GROATS
  CYCLE GUIDE
- ON THE RUFFSTUFF -
  84 BIKE RIDES IN NORTH ENGLAND
- RURAL RIDES NO.1 WEST SURREY
- RURAL RIDES NO.1 EAST SURREY
- SOUTH LAKELAND CYCLE RIDES
- THE WAY OF ST JAMES
  LE PUY TO SANTIAGO - CYCLIST'S

LAKE DISTRICT AND
MORECAMBE BAY
- CONISTON COPPER MINES
- CUMBRIA WAY & ALLERDALE
  RAMBLE
- THE CHRONICLES OF MILNTHORPE
- THE EDEN WAY
- FROM FELL AND FIELD
- KENDAL - A SOCIAL HISTORY
- A LAKE DISTRICT ANGLER'S GUIDE
- LAKELAND TOWNS
- LAKELAND VILLAGES
- LAKELAND PANORAMAS
- THE LOST RESORT?
- SCRAMBLES IN THE LAKE DISTRICT
- MORE SCRAMBLES IN THE
  LAKE DISTRICT
- SHORT WALKS IN LAKELAND
  BOOK 1: SOUTH
  BOOK 2: NORTH
  BOOK 3: WEST
- ROCKY RAMBLER'S WILD WALKS
- RAIN OR SHINE
- ROADS AND TRACKS OF THE
  LAKE DISTRICT
- THE TARNS OF LAKELAND
  VOL 1: WEST
- THE TARNS OF LAKELAND VOL 2:
  EAST
- WALKING ROUND THE LAKES
- WALKS SILVERDALE/ARNSIDE
- WINTER CLIMBS IN LAKE DISTRICT

NORTH-WEST ENGLAND
- WALKING IN CHESHIRE
- FAMILY WALKS IN FOREST OF
  BOWLAND
- WALKING IN THE FOREST OF
  BOWLAND

- LANCASTER CANAL WALKS
- WALKER'S GUIDE TO LANCASTER
  CANAL
- CANAL WALKS VOL 1: NORTH
- WALKS FROM THE LEEDS-LIVERPOOL
  CANAL
- THE RIBBLE WAY
- WALKS IN RIBBLE COUNTRY
- WALKING IN LANCASHIRE
- WALKS ON THE WEST PENNINE
  MOORS
- WALKS IN LANCASHIRE WITCH
  COUNTRY
- HADRIAN'S WALL
  VOL 1 : THE WALL WALK
  VOL 2 : WALL COUNTRY WALKS

NORTH-EAST ENGLAND
- NORTH YORKS MOORS
- THE REIVER'S WAY
- THE TEESDALE WAY
- WALKING IN COUNTY DURHAM
- WALKING IN THE NORTH PENNINES
- WALKING IN NORTHUMBERLAND
- WALKING IN THE WOLDS
- WALKS IN THE NORTH YORK
  MOORS BOOKS 1 AND 2
- WALKS IN THE YORKSHIRE DALES
  BOOKS 1,2 AND 3
- WALKS IN DALES COUNTRY
- WATERFALL WALKS - TEESDALE &
  HIGH PENNINES
- THE YORKSHIRE DALES
- YORKSHIRE DALES ANGLER'S GUIDE

THE PEAK DISTRICT
- STAR FAMILY WALKS PEAK
  DISTRICT/STH YORKS
- HIGH PEAK WALKS
- WEEKEND WALKS IN THE PEAK
  DISTRICT
- WHITE PEAK WALKS
  VOL.1 NORTHERN DALES
  VOL.2 SOUTHERN DALES
- WHITE PEAK WAY
- WALKING IN PEAKLAND
- WALKING IN SHERWOOD FOREST
- WALKING IN STAFFORDSHIRE
- THE VIKING WAY

WALES AND WELSH BORDERS
- ANGLESEY COAST WALKS
- ASCENT OF SNOWDON
- THE BRECON BEACONS
- CLWYD ROCK
- HEREFORD & THE WYE VALLEY
- HILLWALKING IN SNOWDONIA
- HILLWALKING IN WALES VOL.1
- HILLWALKING IN WALES VOL.2
- LLEYN PENINSULA COASTAL PATH
- WALKING OFFA'S DYKE PATH
- THE PEMBROKESHIRE COASTAL
  PATH
- THE RIDGES OF SNOWDONIA
- SARN HELEN

- SCRAMBLES IN SNOWDONIA
- SEVERN WALKS
- THE SHROPSHIRE HILLS
- THE SHROPSHIRE WAY
- SPIRIT PATHS OF WALES
- WALKING DOWN THE WYE
- A WELSH COAST TO COAST WALK
- WELSH WINTER CLIMBS

THE MIDLANDS
- CANAL WALKS VOL 2: MIDLANDS
- THE COTSWOLD WAY
- COTSWOLD WALKS
  BOOK 1: NORTH
  BOOK 2: CENTRAL
  BOOK 3: SOUTH
- THE GRAND UNION CANAL WALK
- HEART OF ENGLAND WALKS
- WALKING IN OXFORDSHIRE
- WALKING IN WARWICKSHIRE
- WALKING IN WORCESTERSHIRE
- WEST MIDLANDS ROCK

SOUTH AND SOUTH-WEST
ENGLAND
- WALKING IN BEDFORDSHIRE
- WALKING IN BUCKINGHAMSHIRE
- CHANNEL ISLAND WALKS
- CORNISH ROCK
- WALKING IN CORNWALL
- WALKING IN THE CHILTERNS
- WALKING ON DARTMOOR
- WALKING IN DEVON
- WALKING IN DORSET
- CANAL WALKS VOL 3: SOUTH
- EXMOOR & THE QUANTOCKS
- THE GREATER RIDGEWAY
- WALKING IN HAMPSHIRE
- THE ISLE OF WIGHT
- THE KENNET & AVON WALK
- THE LEA VALLEY WALK
- LONDON THEME WALKS
- THE NORTH DOWNS WAY
- THE SOUTH DOWNS WAY
- THE ISLES OF SCILLY
- THE SOUTHERN COAST TO COAST
- SOUTH WEST WAY
  VOL.1 MINEH'D TO PENZ.
  VOL.2 PENZ. TO POOLE
- WALKING IN SOMERSET
- WALKING IN SUSSEX
- THE THAMES PATH
- TWO MOORS WAY
- WALKS IN KENT BOOK 1
- WALKS IN KENT BOOK 2
- THE WEALDWAY & VANGUARD WAY

SCOTLAND
- WALKING IN THE ISLE OF ARRAN
- THE BORDER COUNTRY -
  A WALKERS GUIDE
- BORDER COUNTRY CYCLE ROUTES
- BORDER PUBS & INNS -
  A WALKERS' GUIDE

- CAIRNGORMS, WINTER CLIMBS
  5TH EDITION
- CENTRAL HIGHLANDS
  6 LONG DISTANCE WALKS
- WALKING THE GALLOWAY HILLS
- WALKING IN THE HEBRIDES
- NORTH TO THE CAPE
- THE ISLAND OF RHUM
- THE ISLE OF SKYE A WALKER'S
  GUIDE
- WALKS IN THE LAMMERMUIRS
- WALKING IN THE LOWTHER HILLS
- THE SCOTTISH GLENS SERIES
  1 - CAIRNGORM GLENS
  2 - ATHOLL GLENS
  3 - GLENS OF RANNOCH
  4 - GLENS OF TROSSACH
  5 - GLENS OF ARGYLL
  6 - THE GREAT GLEN
  7 - THE ANGUS GLENS
  8 - KNOYDART TO MORVERN
  9 - THE GLENS OF ROSS-SHIRE
- SCOTTISH RAILWAY WALKS
- SCRAMBLES IN LOCHABER
- SCRAMBLES IN SKYE
- SKI TOURING IN SCOTLAND
- THE SPEYSIDE WAY
- TORRIDON - A WALKER'S GUIDE
- WALKS FROM THE WEST HIGHLAND
  RAILWAY
- THE WEST HIGHLAND WAY
- WINTER CLIMBS NEVIS & GLENCOE

IRELAND
- IRISH COASTAL WALKS
- THE IRISH COAST TO COAST
- THE MOUNTAINS OF IRELAND

WALKING AND TREKKING IN THE ALPS
- WALKING IN THE ALPS
- 100 HUT WALKS IN THE ALPS
- CHAMONIX TO ZERMATT
- GRAND TOUR OF MONTE ROSA
  VOL. 1 AND VOL. 2
- TOUR OF MONT BLANC

FRANCE, BELGIUM AND LUXEMBOURG
- WALKING IN THE ARDENNES
- ROCK CLIMBS BELGIUM & LUX.
- THE BRITTANY COASTAL PATH
- CHAMONIX - MONT BLANC
  WALKING GUIDE
- WALKING IN THE CEVENNES
- CORSICAN HIGH LEVEL ROUTE:
  GR20
- THE ECRINS NATIONAL PARK
- WALKING THE FRENCH ALPS: GR5
- WALKING THE FRENCH GORGES
- FRENCH ROCK
- WALKING IN THE HAUTE SAVOIE
- WALKING IN THE LANGUEDOC
- TOUR OF THE OISANS: GR54
- WALKING IN PROVENCE
- THE PYRENEAN TRAIL: GR10
- THE TOUR OF THE QUEYRAS
- ROBERT LOUIS STEVENSON TRAIL
- WALKING IN TARENTAISE &
  BEAUFORTAIN ALPS
- ROCK CLIMBS IN THE VERDON

- TOUR OF THE VANOISE
- WALKS IN VOLCANO COUNTRY

FRANCE/SPAIN
- ROCK CLIMBS IN THE PYRENEES
- WALKS & CLIMBS IN THE PYRENEES
- THE WAY OF ST JAMES
  LE PUY TO SANTIAGO - WALKER'S
- THE WAY OF ST JAMES
  LE PUY TO SANTIAGO - CYCLIST'S

SPAIN AND PORTUGAL
- WALKING IN THE ALGARVE
- ANDALUSIAN ROCK CLIMBS
- BIRDWATCHING IN MALLORCA
- COSTA BLANCA ROCK
- COSTA BLANCA WALKS VOL 1
- COSTA BLANCA WALKS VOL 2
- WALKING IN MALLORCA
- ROCK CLIMBS IN MAJORCA, IBIZA &
  TENERIFE
- WALKING IN MADEIRA
- THE MOUNTAINS OF CENTRAL
  SPAIN
- THE SPANISH PYRENEES GR11
  2ND EDITION
- WALKING IN THE SIERRA NEVADA
- WALKS & CLIMBS IN THE PICOS DE
  EUROPA
- VIA DE LA PLATA

SWITZERLAND
- ALPINE PASS ROUTE, SWITZERLAND
- THE BERNESE ALPS A WALKING
  GUIDE
- CENTRAL SWITZERLAND
- THE JURA: HIGH ROUTE & SKI
  TRAVERSES
- WALKING IN TICINO, SWITZERLAND
- THE VALAIS, SWITZERLAND -
  A WALKING GUIDE

GERMANY, AUSTRIA AND EASTERN EUROPE
- MOUNTAIN WALKING IN AUSTRIA
- WALKING IN THE BAVARIAN ALPS
- WALKING IN THE BLACK FOREST
- THE DANUBE CYCLE WAY
- GERMANY'S ROMANTIC ROAD
- WALKING IN THE HARZ
  MOUNTAINS
- KING LUDWIG WAY
- KLETTERSTEIG NORTHERN
  LIMESTONE ALPS
- WALKING THE RIVER RHINE TRAIL
- THE MOUNTAINS OF ROMANIA
- WALKING IN THE SALZKAMMERGUT
- HUT-TO-HUT IN THE STUBAI ALPS
- THE HIGH TATRAS

SCANDANAVIA
- WALKING IN NORWAY
- ST OLAV'S WAY

ITALY AND SLOVENIA
- ALTA VIA - HIGH LEVEL WALKS
  DOLOMITES
- CENTRAL APENNINES OF ITALY
- WALKING CENTRAL ITALIAN ALPS
- WALKING IN THE DOLOMITES
- SHORTER WALKS IN THE
  DOLOMITES

- WALKING ITALY'S GRAN PARADISO
- LONG DISTANCE WALKS IN ITALY'S
  GRAN PARADISO
- ITALIAN ROCK
- WALKS IN THE JULIAN ALPS
- WALKING IN SICILY
- WALKING IN TUSCANY
- VIA FERRATA SCRAMBLES IN THE
  DOLOMITES

OTHER MEDITERRANEAN COUNTRIES
- THE ATLAS MOUNTAINS
- WALKING IN CYPRUS
- CRETE - THE WHITE MOUNTAINS
- THE MOUNTAINS OF GREECE
- JORDAN - WALKS, TREKS, CAVES ETC.
- THE MOUNTAINS OF TURKEY
- TREKS & CLIMBS WADI RUM
  JORDAN
- CLIMBS & TREKS IN THE ALA DAG
- WALKING IN PALESTINE

HIMALAYA
- ADVENTURE TREKS IN NEPAL
- ANNAPURNA - A TREKKER'S GUIDE
- EVEREST - A TREKKERS' GUIDE
- GARHWAL & KUMAON -
  A TREKKER'S GUIDE
- KANGCHENJUNGA -
  A TREKKER'S GUIDE
- LANGTANG, GOSAINKUND &
  HELAMBU TREKKERS GUIDE
- MANASLU - A TREKKER'S GUIDE

OTHER COUNTRIES
- MOUNTAIN WALKING IN AFRICA -
  KENYA
- OZ ROCK – AUSTRALIAN CRAGS
- WALKING IN BRITISH COLUMBIA
- TREKKING IN THE CAUCASUS
- GRAND CANYON & AMERICAN
  SOUTH WEST
- ROCK CLIMBS IN HONG KONG
- ADVENTURE TREKS WEST NORTH
  AMERICA
- CLASSIC TRAMPS IN NEW ZEALAND

TECHNIQUES AND EDUCATION
- SNOW & ICE TECHNIQUES
- ROPE TECHNIQUES
- THE BOOK OF THE BIVVY
- THE HILLWALKER'S MANUAL
- THE TREKKER'S HANDBOOK
- THE ADVENTURE ALTERNATIVE
- BEYOND ADVENTURE
- FAR HORIZONS - ADVENTURE
  TRAVEL FOR ALL
- MOUNTAIN WEATHER

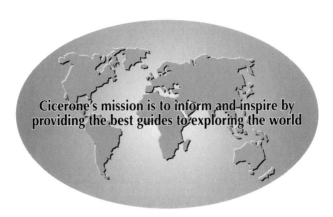

Cicerone's mission is to inform and inspire by providing the best guides to exploring the world

Since its foundation over 30 years ago, Cicerone has specialised in publishing guidebooks and has built a reputation for quality and reliability. It now publishes nearly 300 guides to the major destinations for outdoor enthusiasts, including Europe, UK and the rest of the world.

Written by leading and committed specialists, Cicerone guides are recognised as the most authoritative. They are full of information, maps and illustrations so that the user can plan and complete a successful and safe trip or expedition – be it a long face climb, a walk over Lakeland fells, an alpine traverse, a Himalayan trek or a ramble in the countryside.

With a thorough introduction to assist planning, clear diagrams, maps and colour photographs to illustrate the terrain and route, and accurate and detailed text, Cicerone guides are designed for ease of use and access to the information.

If the facts on the ground change, or there is any aspect of a guide that you think we can improve, we are always delighted to hear from you.

Cicerone Press
2 Police Square Milnthorpe Cumbria LA7 7PY
Tel:01539 562 069   Fax:01539 563 417
e-mail:info@cicerone.co.uk   web:www.cicerone.co.uk

CICERONE